# CAMBRIDGE LIBRARY COLLECTION

*Books of enduring scholarly value*

## Travel and Exploration

The history of travel writing dates back to the Bible, Caesar, the Vikings and the Crusaders, and its many themes include war, trade, science and recreation. Explorers from Columbus to Cook charted lands not previously visited by Western travellers, and were followed by merchants, missionaries, and colonists, who wrote accounts of their experiences. The development of steam power in the nineteenth century provided opportunities for increasing numbers of 'ordinary' people to travel further, more economically, and more safely, and resulted in great enthusiasm for travel writing among the reading public. Works included in this series range from first-hand descriptions of previously unrecorded places, to literary accounts of the strange habits of foreigners, to examples of the burgeoning numbers of guidebooks produced to satisfy the needs of a new kind of traveller - the tourist.

## Geography of Hudson's Bay

The publications of the Hakluyt Society (founded in 1846) made available edited (and sometimes translated) early accounts of exploration. The first series, which ran from 1847 to 1899, consists of 100 books containing published or previously unpublished works by authors from Christopher Columbus to Sir Francis Drake, and covering voyages to the New World, to China and Japan, to Russia and to Africa and India. This volume, published in 1852, was edited by John Barrow, son of the distinguished promoter of Arctic exploration Sir John Barrow. It contains two accounts of exploration around Hudson's Bay – the narrative of Captain William Coats who made several voyages in the region in the 1720s and 30s, and the log of Captain Middleton of H.M.S. *Furnace* who in 1741–2 attempted to discover the much sought-after North-West Passage from the Atlantic to the Pacific. (This was a significant topic in 1852, when the fate of Sir John Franklin's expedition of 1845 was still not known.) A controversy which had arisen between Middleton and the 'projector' of his voyage, a Mr Dobbs, seems to have motivated Coats to write his narrative, as he shows great indignation on behalf of his maligned fellow-captain and pours scorn upon Dobbs for the lack of professionalism with which he treats his sources of information.

Cambridge University Press has long been a pioneer in the reissuing of out-of-print titles from its own backlist, producing digital reprints of books that are still sought after by scholars and students but could not be reprinted economically using traditional technology. The Cambridge Library Collection extends this activity to a wider range of books which are still of importance to researchers and professionals, either for the source material they contain, or as landmarks in the history of their academic discipline.

Drawing from the world-renowned collections in the Cambridge University Library, and guided by the advice of experts in each subject area, Cambridge University Press is using state-of-the-art scanning machines in its own Printing House to capture the content of each book selected for inclusion. The files are processed to give a consistently clear, crisp image, and the books finished to the high quality standard for which the Press is recognised around the world. The latest print-on-demand technology ensures that the books will remain available indefinitely, and that orders for single or multiple copies can quickly be supplied.

The Cambridge Library Collection will bring back to life books of enduring scholarly value (including out-of-copyright works originally issued by other publishers) across a wide range of disciplines in the humanities and social sciences and in science and technology.

# Geography of Hudson's Bay

*Being the Remarks of Captain W. Coats
in Many Voyages to that Locality between
the Years 1727 and 1751*

WILLIAM COATS
EDITED BY JOHN BARROW

CAMBRIDGE
UNIVERSITY PRESS

CAMBRIDGE UNIVERSITY PRESS

Cambridge, New York, Melbourne, Madrid, Cape Town, Singapore,
São Paolo, Delhi, Dubai, Tokyo, Mexico City

Published in the United States of America by Cambridge University Press, New York

www.cambridge.org
Information on this title: www.cambridge.org/9781108008099

© in this compilation Cambridge University Press 2010

This edition first published 1852
This digitally printed version 2010

ISBN 978-1-108-00809-9 Paperback

WORKS ISSUED BY

# The Hakluyt Society.

———◆———

# THE GEOGRAPHY OF
# HUDSON'S BAY.

M.DCCC.LII.

THE

# GEOGRAPHY

OF

# HUDSON'S BAY:

BEING THE

## REMARKS OF CAPTAIN W. COATS,

IN MANY VOYAGES TO THAT LOCALITY,

BETWEEN THE YEARS 1727 AND 1751.

### With an Appendix,

CONTAINING

EXTRACTS FROM THE LOG OF CAPT. MIDDLETON ON HIS VOYAGE FOR
THE DISCOVERY OF THE NORTH-WEST PASSAGE, IN
H.M.S. "FURNACE", IN 1741-2.

EDITED BY

## JOHN BARROW, Esq., F.R.S., F.S.A.

---

" And to speake of no other matter than of the hopefull passage to the north-west: how
many of the best sort of men have set their whole indevours to prove a passage that waye, and
not only in conference, but also in writing, and publishing to the world; yea what great
summes of money hath been spent about that action, as your worship hath costly experience
thereoff."

*Extract of a letter from Baffin to the Right Worshipfull Master John Wolstenholme, Esquire,
one of the chief adventurers for the discoverie of a passage to the north-west.*—HAKLUYT.

---

LONDON:

PRINTED FOR THE HAKLUYT SOCIETY.

M.DCCC.LII.

TO

THE REVERED MEMORY OF THE GOOD

SIR CHARLES MALCOLM, Knt.,

LATE VICE-ADMIRAL OF THE WHITE,

A MAN UNIVERSALLY HONOURED AND BELOVED,

AND ONE OF THE MOST ACTIVE MEMBERS OF
THE HAKLUYT SOCIETY,

This Volume

IS HUMBLY DEDICATED BY HIS FAITHFUL FRIEND,

THE EDITOR.

# INTRODUCTORY REMARKS.

In submitting to the members of the Hakluyt Society
the following " Geography of Hudson's Bay",—being
the " Remarks of Captain William Coats in many
voyages to that locality",—I could wish that it had
fallen into the hands of some one who, with greater
ability and more leisure, would do greater justice in
editing the work, and seeing the manuscript through
the press.

I cannot, however, feel otherwise than flattered at
being invited to edit this Journal, and the more so,
as I consider it a mark of respect to the memory
of my lamented father, who was the fountain-head
of all modern arctic discovery, and whose name is
inseparably connected with everything that relates to
that interesting subject.   On this account principally
the task has been undertaken.

I do not know that it is the bounden duty of an
editor to explain why he considers that the work he
undertakes to edit should be submitted to his readers,
but he may at least crave the indulgence of the
Hakluyt Society, in hoping that a subject which
affords him great delight, may not be altogether

without amusement or instruction to them; and the remarks of Captain Coats seem to be, generally speaking, so judicious throughout, and contain so much valuable information, and such good sound sense, that I trust the members of our Society will hold me excused for submitting them to their perusal.

Captain Coats appears himself to have made many voyages into Hudson's Bay, and to have been twice shipwrecked in the ice on his voyage to the straits; to which events he very concisely thus alludes: once, " in the year 1727, when near the meridian of Cape Farewell, when running through the ice with a small sail, when two pieces of ice shutt upon us, and sunk our ship; and in 1736, being entangled in ice six leagues within Cape Resolution, when the ice shutt upon us, by the tides only (for it was dead calm), and crushed out sides in, and sunk her in twenty minutes."

There is an additional interest, I conceive, attached to the journal of Captain Coats, from the circumstance of its having been drawn up for the use of his sons; and he concludes by saying, that if they are neglected by the Hudson's Bay Company, they are at liberty, and " it is his will and command that every part be made publick, for the use and benefit of mankind." That his remarks should at some future period come to light, it is evident was the wish of Captain Coats, who states, that " he has committed them to writing, least they be buried with him, and posterity be deprived of what may one day be thought of some use."

The hydrographical parts, he says, are " so adjusted and with such care," that he " willingly submits them to the test of time"; and, although a century has elapsed since they were penned, his remarks will be found surprisingly accurate, and well deserving of being perpetuated among the rare and unpublished voyages and travels which the Hakluyt Society is engaged in preserving from the ravages of time.

It will be seen, that in the first page of Captain Coats's manuscript, an allusion is made to the voyage of Captain Middleton to Hudson's Bay in 1741-2, when he discovered the Wager River, and to an unhappy controversy which occurred between Mr. Dobbs, the projector of the voyage, and himself. Wishing to inform myself more particularly of the merits of that voyage, I have referred to the original documents in the archives of the Admiralty, a department under my especial charge. As there is no published account of Captain Middleton's voyage, beyond the log of the *Furnace*, of which I have not been able to find a copy extant, it has occurred to me that the pages of the present number of the Transactions of the Hakluyt Society would be a proper medium to place on record a few facts connected with the voyage of Middleton, extracted from the original manuscripts and log of the *Furnace*, with one or two letters, hitherto unpublished, addressed by Captain Middleton to the Board of Admiralty, together with his " observations while in winter quarters in Churchill River," which I believe have

never appeared in print. These will be found in the
Appendix, and they are of themselves documents containing much interesting matter.

It was not till long after the return of Captain
Middleton from his voyage for the discovery of a
north-west passage through Hudson's Straits, that
this unhappy controversy arose. Captain Middleton
was charged by Mr. Dobbs with neglect, in having
failed to explore the line of coast which afforded a
probability of a passage to the north-west. The principal points at issue appear to have been in respect
to the following discoveries of Middleton, viz., the
Wager River, Repulse Bay, and the Frozen Strait.
As regards the first, Mr. Dobbs asserted that the tide
came through the so-called river from the westward :
but this question was settled the following year by
Captain Moore, who entirely confirmed Captain Middleton's report. Repulse Bay (most appropriately
named, for it sadly repulsed Captain Lyon in the
*Griper* in the year 1824) was no less accurately laid
down by Captain Middleton ; and of the Frozen
Strait, Sir Edward Parry remarks : " Above all, the
accuracy of Captain Middleton is manifest upon the
point most strenuously argued against him, for our
subsequent experience has not left the smallest doubt
of Repulse Bay and the northern part of the Welcome being filled by a rapid tide flowing into it from
the eastward, through the Frozen Strait.

" It was here", observes Sir Edward Parry, " that
Captain Middleton and Mr. Dobbs were most at
issue ; the former asserting, that in his discovery of

the Frozen Strait,[1] through which he actually saw the tide of flood coming into the Welcome, the question was solved in a manner highly conclusive to every unprejudiced mind; while the latter, fully impressed with a conviction, that the story of the Frozen Strait was all a chimera, as well as everything Captain Middleton had said concerning that part of the voyage, confidently insisted on the probability of the tide finding its way through Wager River, or at least through some arm of the sea communicating with that inlet from the westward."

On looking through the correspondence at the Admiralty, it is impossible not to be struck with the straight-forward manliness, candour, and honesty of purpose, exemplified by Captain Middleton throughout this trying business; and no person on perusing the documents can feel otherwise than convinced that it was a cruel attack made by Mr. Dobbs upon the reputation of a skilful and intrepid navigator and an honourable high-minded man. Had my lamented father seen these documents, I am convinced he would have arrived at the same conclusion as myself, and would have done that justice to Captain Middleton which I am proud of this opportunity of handing down to posterity.

That the Lords of the Admiralty were perfectly satisfied with his conduct, there is every reason to suppose, as in the following year he was placed in command of the *Shark* sloop.

[1] " A Vindication of the conduct of Captain Middleton", etc.; London, 1743. Dobbs's " Abstract of Captain Middleton's Journal", etc.; London, 1744.

The difficulties that Captain Middleton had to contend with on his voyage to Hudson's Bay, were great. Many of his men were pressed into the service (a press-warrant having been issued to him); and the description of characters he had to deal with may be judged of from one of his letters, which will be found in the Appendix ; yet, notwithstanding his ill-assorted crew, he did all that it was possible to accomplish, and made many new discoveries, of which the Wager River (named after Sir Charles Wager, then first lord of the Admiralty), was perhaps not the least important.

I hope to be excused for quoting from Captain Middleton's log a few extracts in the Appendix, which will serve to shew how they passed the winter in the ice a century ago,—very different indeed both in the manner and the results to that of the present time, when no less than seven of our ships in search of Sir John Franklin have gone through an arctic winter with the loss of only one man, who "died at his post" from fatigue, while dragging the sledges.[1]

[1] " GEORGE S. MALCOLM, captain of the hold of the *Resolute*, a native of Dundee, whose death was attributed to exhaustion and frostbite, brought on whilst labouring as captain of the sledge *Excellent* (virtually, it may be said), died at his post. He was a most valuable and much respected petty officer. His remains are at rest on the north-east shore of Griffith Island." — *Captain Austin's Dispatch, 12th of August* 1851.

The *Plover*, too (under the command of Captain Moore), has passed three arctic winters within Behring Straits, with the loss of only one man, who died of consumption, and is now passing a fourth winter.

The too liberal supply of spirits is evidently a grievous error; and we shall be curious to see the result of the voyage of Lady Franklin's little vessel, the *Prince Albert*, now passing an arctic winter, which has sailed upon temperance principles, under the command of Mr. Kennedy, accompanied by the brave young French officer, M. Bellot, and the faithful John Hepburn.

In submitting the remarks of Captain Coats, on his voyages to Hudson's Straits, it may not be considered out of place to add a few words in respect to the first establishment of the Hudson's Bay Company, under whom he served for many years.

The original charter granted to the Hudson's Bay Company remains undisturbed, although its validity has of late been much called in question. It was in the year 1668 that Prince Rupert sent an expedition to Hudson's Bay, under the command of Captain Zachariah Gillam, consisting of a small vessel called the *Nonsuch*. They wintered at Rupert's River, and established a fort called Fort Charles, which appears to have been the first English settlement in Hudson's Bay.

A charter having been granted by King Charles, the " Governor and Company of Adventurers of England trading into Hudson's Bay", became the possessors of the land.

Mr. Shillinglaw, in his recently published *Narrative of Arctic Discovery* (a work carefully compiled and of much merit), states " that this charter granted to them and their successors the sole trade and commerce to Hudson's Bay and Straits, with territorial rights and jurisdiction over all the land and countries on the coasts and confines of the same, which were not actually possessed by the subjects of any other Christian prince or state, to be reckoned and reputed as one of the British plantations or colonies in America, under the name of Rupert's Land."

Another clever little work, entitled an *Examination of the Charter and Proceedings of the Hudson's Bay Company, with reference to the Grant of Vancouver's Island* (published in 1849, by Mr. Fitzgerald), contains a minute account of the origin and present position of the Company. To this work I would refer all who wish to investigate the history of their settlements. It contains matter of much serious reflection.

" There is little doubt," as Mr. Fitzgerald observes, " that France laid claim to the Hudson's Bay territories as early as the year 1598, when letters patent were granted by Henry IV of France to Signor de la Roche, appointing him lieutenant-governor over the countries of Canada, Hochelaga, Labrador, and the river of the great Bay of Norrembegne, etc. ; and that the country was, in fact, at one time actually occupied by the French.

" The French Fur Company of Quebec, established forty years before the Hudson's Bay Company, appear to have traversed the whole of the country which the Hudson's Bay Company now claim. For many years, when the English Company never ventured to leave the shores of the Bay, when the whole of their esta-

blishment consisted of four or five insignificant forts
on its shores, the voyagers of the French Company
were traversing the whole of the country north-west
of the Canadas, as far, it is said, as Suskatchewan
River."

Mr. Fitzgerald[1] speaks with much warmth of the
miserable state of thraldom in which the Indian
population has been kept, under the rule of the Company. " Civilization has been to them, not the sun
that warms, but the lightning that scorches; and
under its influence, instead of growing and advancing
in the scale of humanity, the North American Indian
seems to have shrivelled still farther into the very
decrepitude of barbarism." It is to be feared that
this may be the case with some of these tribes; the
Chippeways, for instance, as mentioned by Sir John
Richardson; but it certainly is very far from the
case with other tribes more immediately under their
control; and it is but fair to the Company to quote
the Crees, who, as Sir John Richardson observes,
have been " for more than twenty-six years under the
undivided control and paternal government of the
Hudson's Bay Company, and are wholly dependant
upon them for ammunition, European clothing, and
other things, which have become necessaries. No
spirituous liquors are distributed to them; and school-
masters and missionaries are encouraged and aided
by the Company to introduce among them the ele-
ments of religion and civilization. One village has

---

[1] Fitzgerald's Hudson's Bay Company.

been established near the dépôt at Norway House, and another at the Pas on the Suskatchewan, each having a church and school-house, and a considerable space of cultivated ground. The conduct of the people is quiet and inoffensive. War is unknown in the Cree district ; and the Company's officers find little difficulty in hiring the young men as occasional labourers."[1]

It will not be uninteresting to the readers of this volume to know that the manuscript of " Captain Coats's Remarks" is the property of Sir Edward Parry, who has had it in his possession for many years, and has obligingly allowed the Society to publish its contents. Of the writer of the remarks, the editor can learn but little ; nothing, in fact, is now known of Captain Coats, except that he was in the Company's service as commander of one or other of their ships from 1727 to 1751. His journal, while in command of the *King George*, in the latter year, is the only memorial of him that is to be found at the Hudson's Bay House. That voyage, it appears, was made to Fort Richmond, on the eastern side of Hudson's Bay ; but the journal, I learn, contains nothing beyond the usual occurrences of such voyages.

J. B.

[1] Sir John Richardson's Journal of a Boat Voyage through Rupert's Land.

# GEOGRAPHY OF HUDSON BAY

HAS not been attempted by any person that I know of. The voyages of Hudson,[1] James,[2] Fox,[3] Button,[4] and others, were directed to perticular purposes; and what has past between Mr. Dobbs[5] and C. Middleton,[6] is so full of argument and dispute, that the real geography is neglected—who by atoo eager pursute after truth have out run it, and left it behind —who by atoo ernest contention about it, have rendred it more doubtfull. Notwithstanding there are in that abun-

---

[1] Hudson's *first* voyage for the discovery of the north-west passage was undertaken in the year 1607.

Sir John Barrow, in his " Chronological History of Arctic Regions", speaks of him as an experienced and intrepid seaman, well skilled in the theory and practice of navigation, and in the use of nautical instruments. " It deserves to be remarked," he says, " that he was the first of the northern navigators, and probably the first Englishman, who made observations on the inclination, or dip of the needle."

On this voyage he proceeded north between the coast of Iceland and the east coast of Greenland, and attained the latitude of about 81°.

His *second* voyage was in the year 1608, when he endeavoured to penetrate between Spitsbergen and Nova Zembla.

His *third*, in 1609, upon which occasion he doubled the North Cape, but shortly returned towards Newfoundland, and down the coast of America.

Hudson's *fourth* voyage was in 1610, which was unhappily the last made by this celebrated navigator, on which he discovered the Straits and Bay which bear his name, and which will for ever hand it down to posterity. His crew mutinied, and the captain, his son, and seven men, were cast adrift in a boat amongst the ice, and perished.

[2] In 1631, Captain James proceeded by Hudson's Bay in search of the north-west passage, and was compelled to winter. His crew underwent great sufferings and privations; and the author of the Chronolo-

dance of rubbage and impertinance,[7] some litle matters to our purpose, what remains of the former worthys, has been so curtailed and mutilated, that very little can bee drawn from thence. What Mr. Dobbs has thought fitt to call a discription of Hudson's Bay, is so erronius, so superficial, and so trifling, in almost every circumstance.

So contrary to the experience and concurrent testimony of every person who have resided in that country, or of those who have used it any considerable time, that when it first

gical History says, that the accounts of his voyage may be called a book of "lamentation, and weeping, and great mourning", as it is "one continued strain of difficulties, and dangers, and complainings, from the first making of the sea off Cape Farewell, till his return to the same point."

[3] In the same year (1631), Captain Luke Fox (who had successively urged the desirableness of a new expedition) proceeded in search of the north-west passage, and who, on his return, published his narrative under the name of the "North-West Fox". He appears to have been a strangely conceited man, but of great talent.

His principal discovery was Sir Thomas Rowe's Welcome, and the island of Brooke Cobham, not to omit a small group of islands no less strangely named than "Briggs his Mathematickes". There must have been a deal of humour mixed with his conceit.

[4] In 1612, Sir Thomas Button proceeded to Hudson's Bay on a voyage of discovery, and having discovered the southern part of Southampton Island, to which he gave the name of Carey's Swan's Nest, wintered at Nelson's River, which he discovered, and which afterwards became the principal settlement of the Hudson's Bay Company. He also discovered Mancel, or Mansfield Islands ; and returned to England the following year, having lost several of his men, who died in winter quarters from the extreme cold.

[5] Arthur Dobbs, Esq., was the chief projector of an expedition in 1741 to discover the north-west passage through Hudson's Straits ; and on the return of Captain Middleton from his unsuccessful attempt, it appears that Mr. Dobbs thought fit to attribute the failure of the voyage to some secret understanding between Captain Middleton and the directors of the Hudson's Bay Company ; which led to a lengthened controversy and much animadversion on either side.

[6] Captain Christopher Middleton, who was appointed to the "Furnace" discovery ship in 1741, on the above voyage of discovery.

[7] Not appertaining to the subject.

appeared it was matter of astonishment to all those who may be supposed to be competent judges.

In that discription the interior parts of that wide extended country were, as he tells us, collected from a refugee, a runnagade, an illiterate, and an entire stranger to all, or most of the bordering countrys uppon Hudson's Bay, a French Indian; and as such never did, nor dare any of those ramble beyond the borders of the superior lake, nor trust themselves amongst the hygher tribes of Indians, but was born and bred in the mungril tribes near the inferior lakes on the skirts and borders of Canada, a very Indian without letters, without experience, and without capacity.

The other part of his description is a mean paltry coppy of notes and observations from C. Middleton, extracted without skill, and applyed without judgement.

His industry has been in truth indifatigable; but the mean and contemptable evidences he had for his circumstances are beyond example; nothing, indeed, can demonstrate his own distrust and doubtfulness so effectually; all the monstrous fables of antiquity can hardly parrelel his absurdities; the persons he quotes in support of his geography, are so well known to our people for their incapacity and incompetency in those matters and facts they are brought to support.

That we were all at gaze to know where the farce was to end; such as it is, 'tis the only publick description of that country. But great pity it is that no better pen then mine would undertake to put this geography in a just light, and shew the many naturall advantages might be drawn from the oyl fishery, the oars [ores], minerals, balsums, dye roots, and a greater increase of the furr trade; the great numbers of robust hardy people of God's creatures abandoned and neglected in the grosest idolitry, who otherwise might be usefully employed to the benefitt of others and salvation and wellfare of themselves. I say if such can be found, and what is said here, should rouze any person to this task, it will more then compensite the litle share I have in it.

However, such as it is, you are wellcome to it; would it were better. I am conscious I have wrote both too much and too little to the purpose, and too much beside, in so wide a field, on so fertile a subject. The hydrography is adjusted with the greatest care from Grimington's[1] and my own experience.

What relates to the interior parts are collected from such persons as none that knew them would dispute their candour and capacity, and which alone are my principal motives to commit these remarks to writing, least they be buried with me, and posterity be deprived of what may one day be thought of some use.

The Honourable Hudson's Bay Company, by royall charter, were invested with all the lands and seas within the Streights of Hudson and Bay adjacent, by gift and grant to them and their successors, with the sole property of trade, and with such power and privileges as was never caled in question till very lately, and which has been confirmed in parliment more than once. And who have always resided in London, the metropolis of Great Britton, from whence we sail on the entrence of this voyage.

As all ships are bound to take pilotts from hence to the Downs, or to Orfordness, this part is sufficiently taken care of, and the draugts of the channile of England is enough. I shall begin at Orfordness.[2] . . . . . . . . . . . . . . . . . . . . . . .

Orkney islands are a cluster of islands so high and bold,

---

[1] The editor can trace no clue to this person. Upon inquiry at the Hudson's Bay House, he learns that "no officer of the name of Grimington appears to have been in the Company's service."

[2] Here follow sailing directions of no interest or value, along the east coast of England, passing Flamborough Head, to Buchanness and to the Orkneys.

and the sea so deap, and washed with so violent a tide, that the navigation through these islands has been in a great measure disused (except by persons very well acquainted) untill very lately; add to these the cloudy tempestious weather, which are an appendage to all cape lands, which have not more influence over the direction of the tides in their courses than they have in the direction of the winds, which do not retard nor accelerate the tides more than the tops of those mountains reflect and reverberate the winds in the direction of their courses;[1] these imbarrissments has hitherto deterred many ships from going this convenient way, at the perril and loss of many valueable ships (and especially Danes, Sweeds, and Dutch India men), who, to avoid these islands and the races and tides near them, have been wont to range into the North Sea 100 or 200 leagues more than was necessary in their passage to or from the Western ocean during this tour, are surprised with cloudy or foggy weather; thus under necessity to alter your cours and depend entirely on your dead reckning in shooting through a passage of twenty-eight miles in breadth, from Brassahead in Sheetland, and North Ronalsha in Orkney, or sixty leagues in breadth from Sheetland to the coast of Norway, a distance so inconsiderable after crossing the ocean or traversing many weeks out of sight of land, that every seaman will agree with me, that no ship ought to be hazarded on such precarious circumstances but uppon the last extreamity.

But this extremity is now to be avoided by the indoustry and labour of Mr. Murdock Mackenzie,[2] who has surveyed

---

[1] This is somewhat obscure; but it probably means that the tides rush past the headlands in the same way that the winds rush over the mountain tops,—neither wind nor tide being stopped in their onward progress.

[2] In the year 1750, Mr. Murdock Mackenzie published a large folio, containing eight maps and fourteen pages of letter-press, under the title of "Orcades, or a Geographic and Hydrographic Survey of the Orkney and Lewis Islands—in eight maps, exhibiting the rocks, shoals, set of

these islands, defined these distracted tides, and layd down the depths of water, the places of anchor ground, and how to use or avoid the direct tides, or to back a ship up on the counter tides, with such care and circumspection, and so plain and practicable to the meanest understanding, that it is now not only a safe but most comodius navigation.

What I have to offer is in your approach to these islands; and before you come within the verge of these tides, you ought to be well assured of the land at the distance of four or five leagues (come not near them in a fogg or dark night). You are carefully to avoid the indraughts of those wide mouthed Friths of Pictland,[1] Wistra, and adjacent to North Ronalsha, at and near which places the ocean tides falls into them with asstonishing force, where the small islands, rocks, and points, which obstruct the force and direction of these furious tides, revers a considerable part of those streams.

These counter tides meeting, and in some places joyning those faint streams from the small opnings, are dilated in all directions, into bays, coves, and small outletts, to maintain that equilibrum so naturall to all fluid bodies; but these nicietys are so well defined by that gentleman, that I can ad nothing to his description.

Hoyhead, from whence most ships take their departure, is a promontary of a stupendious height, and may be seen upwards of twenty leagues; is in latitude, 58° 50′ N.;[2] longitude, west from London, 4° 20′ W.; and is a pendent mountain of a reddish coulor, and has thirty fatham water very near its foot.

the tides, etc., interspersed with suitable directions for sailors." A copy of this work is in the Hydrographical Department of the Admiralty.

[1] Pentland.

[2] The latitudes given will generally be found surprisingly accurate, considering the period at which Captain Coats' remarks are written,—the longitudes, of course, less so.

Westwarde, as you sail you meet with two islands caled in the mapps Solesskery, but we name them with others the Stack and Skerry, W. ½ S., eleven leagues from Hoyhead ; the Stack is pritty high and white with fowls' dung, and the Skerry is a low flatt island, N.E. ½ N., three miles asunder, from whence the Orkney people once a year go a seal catching, and to the Stack for eggs, where is vast quantities.

Barra and Rona, are two islands twenty-six leagues from Hoy, W. ½ N., in latitude 59° 05′ N., are high bold land, and are east and west five miles asunder; the eastermost, or Barra, is inhabitted, and in one appearence not unlike a whale uppon the water, with a great diclivity in the middle, where is said to be a small harbour.

St. Kilday are four islands more to westward, in latitude 58° 10′ N.; and longitude, west from Hoy head, 5° 30′ W.; and these are high bold land, the westermost of a pyramidal form like a sugar loaff.

Rokel[1] is a solitary island, in latitude 57° 38′ N.; longitude, west from Hoy head, 10° 30′ W.

Rokele is a piramid not unlike the Stack, but higher and bigger, and white from the same cause ; and I had no ground at eighty fatham on the N.W. side, at the distance of a mile and a half, and I made E. 10° N. erly from this rock to Hoy heade.

Cape Wrathe or Farro head, the north-west promontary of Scotland, lyes twenty-one leagues W.S.W. from Hoy head, in latitude 58° 30′ N. To the eastward, and also to the southward, are mountains of an astonishing height, and the sides near this cape are greatly accelerated ; it bears south-west by south from the eastern Barrow, and five miles more northerly than Gallen head and the Isle of Dunibegg, the northern

---

[1] This may be noticed as a remarkable instance of Captain Coats' accuracy. Rokel (Rockall) is a small rock in the Atlantic, well known to navigators, in latitude 57° 36′ N., longitude 13° 41′ W., as determined by Captain Vidal, R.N., who surveyed it in 1831.

point of Lewis Island, and to eastward forty-two miles ; latitude 58°. 25′ N., and in longitude west from Hoy head thirty-four leagues, or 3° 15′ W. ; or Gallen head, Dunibegg, and the Butt of Lewis, for by all these names it is desined.

Flannen Islands are a small cluster of isles, thirty-four miles to westward of Dunibegg, and eleven to southward, latitude 58° 14′ N. ; which in cloudy weather I have more than once taken for St. Kilday's islands, but can be of no ill consequences, the islands and highlands are so bold and high. At twenty leagues distance, to westward of St. Kilday, you have soundings from ninety to forty fathom. With these helps and these situations, how facile and easy is it.

Coming in for the land from the Western Ocean, I came out of the North Sea sumwhat abruptly into the ocean, lead by my subject, insensible being. I would give you the lands and islands togeather in the trackt of foreign ships ; but if you are going to southward through the highlands to Ireland or the western ports of Brittain, the islands are innumerable, the tides are so powerfull and so distracted, that none but a person sufficiently acquainted are capible to take charge of a ship.

An therefore crave leave, before I take my departure, to inform my reader that in the Bay and Frith of Murray are two principle harbours, at Cromertie and Channery, near the Codd, fitt for any ships to put into, and severall small places on either shore, not worth and beside our purpose.

Orkney Islands abounds with so many fine roads and safe harbours, that it may not improperly be caled a port of harbours sufficiente to shelter and secure all the ships of the known world, and is so com̄odiusly situated for the northern navigation, that I am surprized it has not been used more in the warr, more esspecially with any of the southern as well as northern powers of Europe.

By its situation is a natural frontier to the Brittish dominions, and is so conveniently situated to cover those parts with a small force, that I am astonish't the government never establish't a rendivouz at these islands, when three or four ships stationed there are capible to give convoy to every ship that goes that way to auw and influence that restless part of the king's dominions, and be always within a day's sail of her station.

These reasons induced me to lay this matter before a publick board, who were so well satisfied that they. immediately made a contract to victuall his majesties navy at this place ; but the peace of Aix-la-Chapelle, in 1748, rendred this useless. But as we seamen say, 'tis good policy in a calm to provide for a storm, so it would be a good precaution for the government to remove those objections which at present make it very (at least expensive) but almost impracticable.

Orkney, by its situation, is capible to shutt up all the ports of the Baltic, and Holland, and Norway, save two places, and even those may be occupied with precariousness and hazard. And our navy never above half a days sail from her rendivouz.

As this is no extravigant supposition, I assert it may be done with more facility than to shutt up the streights of Dover, and with less hazard and danger to our heavy ships (for in these seas we have no want of water) ; we are scarce fifty leagues from the coast of Norway to Yell, and Unst, and the Skerrys, that not a boat can pass without our knowledge. And while the nation has a Hawk, or Anson, or a Warren, we have but to see and conquer.

And I am so convinced of the practableness of this measure, that I flatter myself it will one day be put in practise ; for I have no end to serve, no intrest to cultivate, and which are the pure dictates of my own experience comitted to writing, as all my other remarks are, as my real sentiments, for the use of my sons.

These sentiments, I must confess, has given me, during

the war, some uneasiness, to observe what high premiums for assurancis and the many lossis of our ships, whereby the trade to the grand metropolis is in a manner destroyed, and estranged to the out ports, when so small a force as this station require, would have given a safe and sure convoy to every ship without going fifty leagues out of her station.

Mr. Mackenzie will pardon me if I give the preference to Holm Sound and Hoy Sound for these reasons : 1st, You have anchor ground al the way through the islands into the Western Ocean, the tides are not so strong, and in the narrow, where you must engage with the Stroom, as they call it, the distance inconsiderable ; add to this, 'tis a shorter cutt in rounding a cape land, where a little time produces great alterations of wether, which in these sounds you may take or leave, go on or stand still.

In Pictland frith and wide away, you have but in some places anchor ground ; you 'r forced to face those furious tides a considerable distances, very deep water ; but in the Stroom no stopping at anchor if you are bafled by the wind, as the hills turn them in all directions, and you should loss the benefitt of backing on the tide in those counter currents, you are drove to westward and eastward alternately, without being able to do one usefull or prudent thing without a stout breeze of wind,—a fickle lady that no well-bred seaman will trust too.

And therefore, as we have gone with convoy all the warr, we have not scruples to go with forty guns ships through those sounds only preferable to any other.

Being now to take my departure in order to sail across the ocean to Hudson's Streights, we confine our selves to the parallels of latitudes 60°, 59°, 58°, 57°, 56°, indifferently, as the wind and weather presents, in which we find a languid current sett to southward, and inclined to westward, of six, eight, or nine mile a day, to the 45° of longitude west from London, at and near the meridian of Cape Farewell, whose latitude, by many observations, is 59° 40′ N.;[1] from thence to Cape Warwick, on the south part of Resolution I'les, in latitude, by observation, 61° 21′ N., is 19° 30′ W. longitude, together is, from London to Resolution on the north entrance, 64° 30′ W. We make this longitude home always, but seldom make above 63° 30′ W., outward bound, which I always attributed to the current aforesaid.

When we approach the meridian of Cape Farewell, we dilate to southward into 58°, or further, to avoid ice, which hang near the verge of the cape most of the summer; for the same reason, we take care to gett up to northward into 61° 30′ north latitude when past that cape, to avoid ice, and a more sensible current near the Labradore coast. The land is very mountainous; but, as it is lined with ice all the summer, we can say but little about it. Cape Farewell is so high, that the snow never all melts off. By other remarks, the longitude of the Cape of Resolution[2] approximated from London 65° 47′ W.; but in the ordinary practice, we make 3° 45′ of longitude more home than in the outerbound passage, so that we make approximated, in outerward bound from London, 63° 55′ W.; in our homeward bound from London, 67° 40′ W.; Resolution to Silly, in many voyages, 59° 00′ E.

Remarks in 1741.—" Says I made 58° W. longitude from Hoyhead to Resolution; and that he had considered the errors in latitude southerly during a passage of twenty-one days; and that the current, according to the strictest cullation, appears to me near the S.W. in its direction, and force, about four miles and a half a day: and he says he is perswaded, that when this allowence is digested in the log, it will reconcile the outerbound with the homewardbound journal." However, this is to be understood, that you sail in those parrelells, for in going south about, this current be-

---

[1] Cape Farewell is in latitude 59° 49′ N.
[2] Cape Resolution is in latitude 61° 30′, longitude 64° 30′ W.

comes quite insinsible ; likewise, if you should be delayed any extraordinary time near the coast of Labrodore, or longer in crossing from Cape Farewell to Resolution, in both cases you meet a southerly current, of at least ten mile a day ; and near that coast, I am of opinion, that current dilates itself to eastward (this remark was confirmed in 1749, of four miles and a half a day).

You are carefully to avoid being entangled in ice before you have enter'd Hudson's Streight.   Ice without is so hardned and wash'd, that it becomes like solid stone ; and as the sea is more open, so you have a swell runs many miles into it ; add to this the tides and currents, which keep it in perpetual motion, that make it very dangerous to hazard a ship amongst it, before yon get into the streights at least twelve or fifteen leagues.  This experience I bought very dear, for in the year 1727, near the meridian of Cape Fare-well, we were worming through ice with a small sail, when two pieces of ice shutt uppon us, and sunk our ship : and in the year 1736, being entangled in ice six leagues within the Cape Resolution, the ice shutt upon us by the sides only (for it was dead calm at the time), and crush'd our sides in, and sunk her in twenty minutes, notwithstanding all our endea-vours.  But as to the method and manner in working amongst ice, I have spoke so largly to it in another place, that I shall refer you to that description.[1]

---

[1] Sir Edward Parry, in his " Journal of a second voyage for the dis-covery of a north-west passage in the years 1821-3," makes the following observations on entering the straits, coinciding remarkably with those of Captain Coats :—" The effects to be apprehended from exposure to the swell of the main ocean constitute the peculiar danger of first entering the ice about the mouth of Hudson's Straits, which is completely open to the influence of the whole Atlantic.  A very inconsiderable quantity of loose ice is sufficient to shelter a ship from the sea, provided it be closely packed ; but when the masses are separated by wind or tide, so as to admit the swell, the concussions soon become too violent for a ship, strengthened in the ordinary way, to withstand for any length of time. On this account it is prudent not to enter the ice without a fair prospect of getting seven or eight leagues within the margin."

Hudson's Streights is a passage of twelve leagues wide at the mouth, formed by a cluster of islands, in latitude 60° 45′ N.; caled Button's Iles and Resolution Iles, before described as the streights, dilates its self immediately on the north side to northward, so on the south side it hold on near that parralel about twenty leagues, and then turns round Amocomancka to southward, and there forms a great bay of fifty leagues from east to west.

Near seventy leagues up the sea turns short up to the northward on the south side and makes a second narrow of seventeen leagues wide, near Savage Point, on the north shore, from whence both shores dilate themselves to westward, and the north side declines more northerly up to Cape Diggs, a cluster of isles on the south side ; latitude 62° 40′ N.; over against which, on the north side, is a passage of at least twenty-five leagues, where you enter the streights from Hudson's Bay from the westward.

As the tides enter these streights from the eastward, so it is most furious about that narrow entrence, but is greatly abated when it comes to be dilated in that great bay to southward; but in the second narrow it is accumilated, and is so increased, that it is very troublesome all the way to Cape Diggs, and over to the island of Mansfield,[1] where it becomes insinsible; it rises near thirty foot on an ordinary spring tide all along the streights, but gradually decreases as you go to westward; and the time of full sea on the full and change is from seven o'clock at Resolution to eleven o'clock at Cape Diggs, and the times and distances corresponds so stricktly in all the intermediate places, that I was asstonisht when I came to consider them, as I have the flowings at many places to compare with. I dont recollect an instance of the like in the geography of the known world. On both sides is lined in most places with numberless nameless islands, where doubtless is many fine harbours; those of

---

[1] Now called Mansell Island.

note, and which we are better acquainted with, after you pass'd into the streights above Button's Islands, four principle in number, but any lesser a high bold land, but wash'd by a violent tide, as is Resolution on the northern side.

Amocomanko,[1] a large bold island on the south side, about twenty leagues to westward of Button's Iles, lyes near a promontary,[2] which makes one side of the bay caled Hope, advanced where the coast dilate to southward.

Plain and Grass Islands.[3] These are two solitary iles which ly before that great bay at some distance from the main, but as we seldom go or come on that side of the streights, I shall haisten to the north shore.

Lower Savage Islands, are three larger, and many lesser, about thirteen leagues above the Cape of Resolution, W.N.W. ½ N., nearest eastermost of which, in latitude 62° 05′ N.

Nix Compestress, or the snowy land, is twenty-eight leagues from the Cape of Resolution. Here the tides are more still and quiet, and not so rude or troublesome as lower down, when incumberd with ice.

Near this place is an iland neat, caled Sadle Back, near the shore, which we have thought may be a good harbour, but never was experienced.

Middle Savage islands are a cluster of islands forty-two leagues from the Cape of Resolution, W.N.W., and ly of from the main six or seven mile,—affords a fine sound between those and the land, but never experienced, for reasons best known to the honourable Hudson's Bay Company.

Ice Cove is a most safe harbour, nine leagues to the W.N.W. of the Great Middle Savage island, and good anchor ground, where I sheltered our ship from ice when I was hard press't; it flowed (nine o'clock) full and change, and

---

[1] Called Akpatok Island in the present charts.
[2] Bay of Hope's Advance.
[3] Now called Green Islands.

rose twenty-eight foot water ; 'tis barren and stoney, scarce any green thing grows uppon the islands. Where we lay we had many Usquemows[1] came and traded with us, which might be improved if the company thought fitt.

Gray Goose island, within which is fine anchor ground, and you ly cover'd from all wind ; but the tides both ways carry the ice through, which is the reason why I think Ice Cove preferable, being is all ways still : and this island is about half way to Ice Cove from Middle Savage isles.

North Bay, or the White Streights. The shore, a little to westward of Ice Cove, declines to northward, and forms this bay or mouth of this streight, by op'ing a passage to northward of Savage Point of at least seven leagues wide, and so extends it self to westward nearly parrellel to Hudson's Streights.

White Streights has sundry i'sles lye in the entrāce from both sides, which do occupie so great a part of the channile that the tides are greatly accelerated. This streights, above thirty leagues from Savage Point, appears through some scattered i'sles we perceived on the north shore, where we found so strong an indraught that with some difficulty we got clear : one of our ships was so entangled, that it cost him eight or ten days in some extreamity with ice and land, before he got out. Thus, while the sea was covered with ice at both places, we could define the sea, which expanded itself, out of sight to the northward, and to all appearance as wide as Hudson's Streights : we had a regular ebb and flood and stout tide, and flows nine and a half hours full and change. We lay inclosed in ice some fourteen days, that our men went every day on the mountains to look for water, who constantly affirmed that this new streight was as boundless as the other.

I the rather call it a straight, for this reason : was it a bay

---

[1] The common appellation for the Esquimaux amongst all the whalers of the present day is " Huskies".

only, the tides would be retarded, not accelerated, as we found by experience ; and the ice as rude and troublesome as in any part of streights ; and it abounds more with i'les of ice than in other places, insomuch that it 'has been said all our i'les of ice come from this streight.

Savage Point, from what has been said, appears to be a large island, with those we call the Upper Savage Islands, forms a promontory. We steer for both ways, and where Hudson's Streights dilate to northward in going up, as it declines more to eastward in going down, whose latitude by many observations 62° 20′ N.  It is west, from the Cape of Resolution, sixty-three leagues. It is east, from the east end of Cape Charles, thirty-two leagues. It is east from Cape Diggs sixty-nine leagues.

I'ts name is disputed, which is all I have to add : some call it God's Mercys : and the Savages islands is farther to east ward ; for my own part, this is the name I received from my predecessors, and until I have reason to alter it shall distinguish it by that name.

Prince Henrys Foreland is a high mountain, ouer against Savage Point, on the south, or Labrodore, at the distance of seventeen leagues from which the land falls away both to southward and northward ; 'tis lined with numberless nameless islands and very rocky, and very deep water near the shore.

False Charles is a promontary, twenty-one leagues to westward of Savage point, and near the same latitude (62° 20′ N.), nine leagues to eastward of Cape Charles. This land we have, in very hazy wether, taken to be Cape Charles some times, from its likeness,—whence its name.

By another minute, the entrance into Hudson's Streights is some twelve leagues wide over to Buttons I'les, which are four in number, large, and divers small ones in the skirts and borders of the Labradore, near Cape Chidley, in latitude 60° 50′ N., and bears from the south point of the I'le of

Resolution, called Cape Warwick,[1] S.E. by S., and are four miles distant from Cape Chidley ; after you pass into the streights about thirty leagues, it dilates, to southward, into a great bay fifty leagues wide : but as our navigation calls us to northward on two occasions, I shall only remark that about      [2] leagues up, the shore turns short up to north-ward, and forms a second narrow, about sixteen or seventeen leagues wide, and so continues gradually widening up to Cape Charles, which is ninety-six leagues to westward of Resolution, and is in 62° 55′ N. latitude, over against which the streights is twenty leagues wide ; beyond this, and up to Cape Diggs, or Digg's I'les, thirty-two leagues, to westward of Cape Charles, lenth of the island included ; makes the whole lenth of the streights, from the eastermost part of the I'les of Resolution to the westermost I'le of Diggs, a hundred and thirty-two leagues, whose latitude is 62° 40′ N. ; differ-ence of longitude, 14° 0′.

And now give me leave to expatiate a litle uppon the great influence this position of the streights has uppon the tides, where the shores accumilate and gather their streams in order to discharge them more forcibly into the mouth of the streights, which is again reiterated and gathered, as in a bagg, in that great bay to southward, in order to restore that languar it would suffar in passing that great distance from the ocean ; and thus made the agent of the distruction and disolution of those tremendious bodys of ice, the seas disin-cumbred, and the seasons alternately restored.

This phenomenon appears to me so providential, that I cannot conceive how this could have been effected without this extrodinary power and force of the tides, considering what prodigious floats of ice are all the summer in these streights, so compact and solid, and made for duration, which, like a common sewer, receives it from all the fuers and bays

---

[1] Now called Hatton's Headland.
[2] Left blank in the manuscript (say sixty).

3

as fast as it is detached by the land-waters and dissolved snow.

I must remark that the northern side of streights and northern parts of the bay, are generally cleared of ice first ; but whether it is owing to more frequent northerly winds in the spring of the year, or a greater quantity of snow, or to an attraction of the luminaries, or all together, this is certain, there is a draining current always to southward, although the winds sometimes produce a contrary effect.

The strange and powerfull effects of the ice is so inter-woven with those violent tides you meet with in your approach to Hudsons Streights, that 'tis not possible to define one without explaining the other, and therefore I judge it neces-sary to observe the particulars following, viz. :

After your ship is well fitted with stores and provisions, according to your number of men, you must add about one fourth more than the ussial allowance in other voyages, pro-vide a stock of ice geer, viz., six ice hooks for mooring, and four or six lesser ones for warping, which will be found extremely usefull ; four ice ropes of thirty or forty fathom each, your buoy ropes, and four whale lines of $2\frac{1}{2}$ inches, with what helps may be made beside ; twelve ice poles, twelve handspikes extrodinary, one dozen long-mouthed wood axes, two or three broad-mouthed chizzells fitted on poles, six boat hooks. I have made upwards of twenty voyages without a small ice-boat, yet I do not deny the use of them.

Thus equiped, you are to sail from England by the 20th of May, in order to be at the mouth of Hudsons Streights by the 6th of July, a few days sooner or later, as the season will admit. I must take notice, that on the 3rd of July in the year 1736, we found the ice so large in the entrance, that, being inclosed, we had our ship crushed to pieces ; and in the year 1739 we attempted to enter the streights six times between the 1st of July and the 12th, and could not effect it, so compact and close a body of ice lay across the entrance, which obliged us to stand out to sea. 'Tis true, sometimes, in favourable seasons, we have entred the streights sooner. I remember once we got in by the 26th of June, and got up, with great labour, about sixty leagues; but there we found such banks and walls of ice from side to side, that we did litle or nothing untill the 20th July; and therefore you see 'tis to litle purpose to be there sooner, and your hazard is much greater, being the ice is more compact, much larger, and not so mashed and shattered; and 'tis incredible what an alteration the spring tides in the beginning of July makes amongst the ice in the mouth of the streights, and what immense bodys it will shatter and breek in shivers, which before was dreadful to look at when agitated and put into motion by those furious tides, which are so distracted and cut by those heavy sands of ice which makes them boyl up in edies and whirlpooles in a most amazing manner, which you are particularly and carefully to attend too; and if you are doubtfull of being intangled before you can get in at least fifteen leagues, and more esspecially on the approach of the springs, you are to forbear, and make it a rule to stand out to sea clear of that indraught.

Further up the streights we find tho ice not so rude, without you are near the shore, or near the i'les of ice, untill you are half way up the streights; and beyond that, to Cape Diggs, in the second narrows, uppon the turns of the tides, and more esspecially on the springs tides, every where the ice is rude and troublesome, and very dangerous.

You must constantly watch its motion, which is strangely affected by the different setts of the tide, and sudden gushes which boils through the different rands, and different species of ice (if I may be allowed the expression), to explain my meaning herein, it may not improperly be divided into three speices of ice, viz. :

First, is those i'les of ice, are such immense bodys, are so deep immersed in the water, below the current of the tides, and are so fixed like land, without motion, or what is scarce sensible.

Second, it is what is called large, heavy, solid ice, and is that specie we must dread to fall amongst. This ice lyes very deep in the water, and feels the full force and power of the tides; these plough and smash the small ice in so an amazing manner, as if God had endowed them with a furious spirit of perdition; and these are so rent and shattered themselves, when they are hurled against those i'les of ice, or one another, as if they strove which should be first disolved.[1]

Third, the small ice is, as it were, the sport of the other two specie of ice, and is much more affected by the winds than by the tides; and this specie is by much the greatest quantity. In and amongst this we always endeavour to shelter our ships, where we ly easy, and quiet, and safe, and undisturbed; but only when we drive near one or other of the other two species of ice, you observe a discomposure, a justling, clashing, and running one against another, as I before mentioned. This is very evident, whether you see them or not, as we have abundance of dark foggy wether.

Thus you see, my sons, how signally providentialy God has ordered the different seasons; with how small an instrument he can compass his intentions. That second specie of ice which is so compact and hard, and to all appearance made for duration, no Portland stone seemingly harder, yet

[1] Purchas, who "out of a chaos of confused intelligences", framed what he calls "his Pilgrimes", thus dilates upon the same subject :— " Nor the unequall seas, which might amaze the hearer, and amate the beholder, where the Tritons and Neptune's selfe would quake with chilling feare, to behold such monstrous icie ilands, renting themselves with terrour of their owne massiness, and disdayning otherwise both the sea's sovereigntie, and the sunne's hottest violence, mustering themselves in those watery plaines where they hold a continual civill warre, and rushing one upon another, make windes and waves give backe ; seeming to rent the eares of others, while they rent themselves with crashing and splitting their congealed armours."—*Purchas his Pilgrimes.*

by lying deeper in the water than the small ice, and not so deep as the i'les of ice, is by the tides made the instrument of disolution, of its self and all the rest.

And so the seasons and returns are provided for ; the seas are kept cool, without being perpetually congealed or incumbred ; and the numerous inhabitants of oyl fish, amphibious creatures, and animals who require cool climes, are accomidated : for 'tis to be noted that the seas are not more affected by the cold ice floating up and down all the summer, than the adjacent coast.

And you may form a pretty true judgment by the appearance of the land, wether their is any ice near it or no, but also according to the quantity. Appears a white gleam over the land and ice in that part where you will perceive the black vapour of the sea alternately chequer the appendant hemisphere ; and this, if carefully attended to, may be perceived to a great distance. The use is too evident to animadvert thereon.

I must not omitt to remark that altho the ice is, as it were, the sport of the tides, yet the tides are violently affected by those thick, heavy, deep rands of ice, which distract them in all directions and in all gradations, according to the bulk and depth they are immersed.

These, as before, plough through the small ice with an asstonishing force, but are overcome by the superior quantity of small ice. In all these encounters there is great danger to be catched near the borders, where the undertow is so powerfull, like falling athwart a tire of ships in a strong tides way. No power can remove untill the return of the contrary tide, and so you ly exposed to the crush and shock of all that comes : these we call escapes with some propriety.

What I have said hitherto principly belongs to the ice in the streights where the tides are powerfull every where ; but the ice in the bay, untill you are near the land, is very still, and is in a manner moved by the winds only ; which makes

us take any method, or sail almost any distance, rather than
fasten in the bay ice. And as a memento, never enter a
body of ice in the night, nor in a fogg, where their is any
hazard of being inclosed, nor before you have circumscribed
it as much as possible; nor imagine 'tis lost time to take two
looks before you resolve once. I have constantly experienced this, which has more than once given me considerable
advantages over other ships; in short, whenever I slighted
this precaution, I generally was punished in the neglect of
it before I got disentangled. Thus much for the ice.

The tides about England are so well defined, that I am
unable to add any great matter thereto, wherr all along the
eastern coast is a regular tide and half tide propogated from
the northern floods, and are accelerated, or retarded, according to the diversity of the shores, or gulphs, or flatts, or
shoalds, or capes, alternately. And here it may be necessary
to explain what I mean by tide and half-tide. Tides, in
their duration, under the influence of the luminaries, undisturbed by winds, neither accelerated nor retarded by the
position of the coasts, bays, shoals, nor other circumstances,
is six hours flood and six hours ebb, correspondent to the
quadratures of the moon; but this influence so impressed on
a fluid body in motion, will continue to run three hours
longer, but not rise higher; and so, *vice versus,* it will run
longer than low water, and not ebb lower; and this motion
is as uniform as the tides, and ebbing and flowing of the sea.
Near great rivers, in bays, shoalds, and other circumstances,
this motion is repulsed, and it is entirely effected in equili-
brio only. That the tides are generated by the influence
of the luminaries, and formed into streams by the continents
reverberating those faint tremours, is demonstrable, from
that great diversity we collect from the different times and
heights of the tides in sundry places, entirely occasioned by
the many obstructions, or gredily swallowing them up, as is
before observed, in their winding courses, round cape lands

or wide mouthed rivers, over long flatts, over shallows, amongst shoalds and ilands, and the like ; for from the North Cape, in Norway, to Cape Bona Esperanza, where the coast lyes open to the ocean, a N.E. and S.W. moon makes full sea every where ; at Whale Cove, a W.S.W. moon makes full sea.

Thus has the wise Author of Nature provided for the wellfare of his creatures in raising so stupendious a fabrick as the tides are, which are not more useful for the business of navigation, than for the salutary refreshments of all nature (thus are they preserved sweet, thus made potable) ; thus, being agitated, are more easily evaporated and barreled up in clouds, and by their appendage the winds are wafted into the thirsty inland countrys.

From the Orkneys to Cape Farewell, we observe, from well-grounded experience, is a S.W. current ; this, as it differs, so is it difficult to define. However, all our corrections is this way : to westward of Cape Farewell the current is southerly ; near the Labrodore, I have known it to set twenty mile a day by observation, and therefore 'tis a caution not to approach too near the coast of Labrodore before you are well to northward in latitude 61° 25′ N., in order to avoid that current, as well as the ice which lyes along that coast all the summer. And for this reason we give Cape Farewell a birthe of a degree of latitude or more, in order to avoid the ice off that cape.

Thus I have brought you, my sons, to the mouth of Hudsons Streights, where great caution is to be taken before you enter. Your ice geer is to be made ready, ruther chains and ruther takles reeved, lighter tacks and sheets for your sails ; and, in short, whatever will make your ship handy.

The tides you shall meet here are so violent and surprising, esspecially when disturbed and distracted by ice, as I before observed in my description of the ice, that nothing but experience can comprehend or imagine. Suppose a ship attempting to strike a tangent across the sterlings of London bridge uppon a strong ebb tide, where the points of these are not more shocking than the points of those, take head how you touch; the undertow nales you fast, and all your efforts are insufficient to disintangle you, and therefore the high and low water slacks are what, with most safety, may be used; and on the appearance of the ice's motion, you are to forsake the water, and push into small ice. I have more than once preserved the ship by this precaution.

The times and heights of the tides are next to be regarded, which enter the streights from the eastward with great force, and an E.S.E. moon makes full sea at Resolution I'les up forty-five leagues; at Midle Savage Islands, S.E. by E. moon makes full sea, and rises thirty foot water.

At Upper Savage Islands, a S.E. moon makes full sea, and rises twenty-four foot water.

At Mill Islands, a S.S.E. moon makes full sea, and rises twenty foot water.

At Seahorse Point, a S. by E. moon makes full sea, and rises eighteen foot water.

At Mansfield Island a S. by E. moon makes full sea, and rises twelve foot water.

At Carieswansnest, a S. by W. moon makes full sea, and rises but six foot water.

Extracts from my journal, 1748:

At Ice Cove, a S.E. moon makes full sea, and rises twenty-eight foot water, and runs half-tide one mile from the shore; 'tis probable all over the streights it may do the same.

And at Bonds Inlet, a S. by E. moon makes full sea, and rises sixteen foot water.

This is a carefull deduction of the tides, where the distances correspond with the tides to a prodigious niceity; and that it is demonstrable the eastern tide spends itself, and is spent, at or near Carieswandnest, nor is there any sensible tide to westward of Mansfield.

How are those lost streems at Carieswansnest accumilated in their progress to the west main? how generated? how formed into tides so powerfull and so strong as they are in all parts of Sir Thos. Roe's Wellcome? is a problem as difficult as it is curious. That these lost streems are propogated in tremours by the impulse of the sun and moon, and are reverberated by the shores, and so formed into tides so powerfull and so strong, will not, cannot be admitted, and yet there is such a conformity and correspondence between the times of full sea and the distances, as leave it extremely doubtful.

If you should grant that there is a western tide, and that, from many circumstances, all along the western shore there is great probability, as will pretty plainly appear when we come to make our deduction of that tide, and how it conformes and corresponds with its times and distances, and that all northerly and westerly winds do considerably rase those tides on the western shore, and that all southerly and easterly do alternately flatt those tides, yet 'tis matter of astonishment that the western tide in James Bay, and the eastern tide[1] at Carieswansnest, nearly on the same meridian, should have high water at one and the same time; and these, in our supposition, propogated from distant and different oceans. I say it is not impossible but it may be so; but it is very remarkable.

You have something like this in the chanile of England tide from the westward, which sweeps the coast of France, Flanders, and Holland, and so far as the Elb to northward.

Notwithstanding, at the same time, a brisk tide comes from the northward, washes all the eastern coasts of Scotland

---

[1] The idea of a western sea seems to have occupied the mind of Captain Coats; which the flood-tide sweeping round the western side of Hudson's Bay would encourage, by making it perhaps appear in James's Bay that the flood came from the westward.

and England as far as Dungenness, and that also there may be some difference in the forces and strenth of those tides, as well as in their times of high water. Yet we are certain they are both propogated and derived from the northern and western flood.

To apply what has been said. It appears to me to be extremely difficult to determine this matter, and shall content myself with giving you the matter of fact, as I have collected them from the experience of others and myself. A bare deduction of the Bay tide shews it in the fullest light, viz. :

In the dispute between A. Dobbs and Captain Middleton, near the latitude of 66° 30′ N., in Sir Thomas Roe's Wellcome, and near the meridian of Cape Southampton, 'tis said a W. by N. moon makes full sea, and setts from the S.W. according to Dobbs ; a west moon, according to Middleton, and comes from the N.E.; and this matter of fact is canvissed with some heat on both sides.

Mr. Dobbs says, if he grants Middleton his postulatum, it will embarriss him, and in his deduction of the times and heiths taken at other places, will reduce him to an absurdity, for if you should give Middleton a point or two of the compass in deducing his tides, it will be of no service to him to support a N.E. tide from his frozen streights, where it will appear from his own deduction, and in his printed mapp, to be directly contrary to matter of fact ; so notorious a trip in him as will justifie all Dobbs has imputed to him ; and this will stand as a monument of folly to posterity, how all attempts to hide the truth are weak and vain.

Mr. Dobbs deduction is naturall and easy, and is supported by matter of fact, viz. :

At Wager River or Streight, a W. by N. moon makes full sea, and rises thirteen foot at an ordinary tide.

And comes from the south west ; for if it came from the frozen streights, it would undoubtedly sweep round his Repulse Bay, where, on the contrary, Middleton lost all appearance of a tide, not only in the force, but height of the tides ; and what is still more notorious, that in the streight near Cape Dobbs, where the sea was squeazed in, it would be accelerated, not languish, as he found it ; and it is beyond all controversy, and he himself agrees, that at or near Brook Cobham he found it flow'd more water, and run stronger, than on any other part of that coast. Cast your eye on the mapp, and see how a N.E. tide could perform this after passing thro that frozen streight, a diminutive stream of a few leagues in breadth, to fill up that wide expanse and run with that force we find them all along the western shore.

At Brook Cobham and Whale Cove, from the authority of Fox, Kelso, Napper, and myself, all our journals assert a W.S.W. moon makes full sea, and rises from fourteen to eighteen foot water.

At Churchill River, a W.N.W.$\frac{1}{2}$N. moon makes full sea, and rises fourteen foot water.

At Port Nelson Shoalds, N.W. by W. moon makes full sea, and rises fourteen foot water.

At Port Nelson Rivers mouth and Hays River mouth, a N.W. moon makes full sea, and rises sixteen foot water.

At Albany Road, a N. or S. moon makes full sea, and rises eight foot water at an ordinary tide.

At Moose River Road S.$\frac{1}{2}$E. moon makes full sea, and rises seven foot at an ordinary tide.

These times and these heights are to be understood when the tides are unincumberd by ice, uninfluenced by high winds, both which make some alteration ; but down James Bay, where the tides are languid, the northerly and westerly winds will bring twelve and fourteen foot water. At York Fort I have known it rise twenty foot ; at Churchill, sixteen foot, which demonstrate that the angular position of the land and coast, and high winds, have a prodigious influence on the natureall course of the tides.

Thus you may observe that the eastern tide spends itself, and is spent, in passing through Hudsons Streights from the oceon to Carieswansnest, nearly two hundred leagues; also the western tide spends itself, and is spent, in passing from Whale Cove to Albany River and Moose River, about two hundred leagues likewise. This congruity of the times of full sea, in this deduction, is indisputable; and I must confess it seems to intimate as if it was all an eastern tide, and I should very readily have come into this sentiment, if I had not, in my last voyage, had entire satisfaction to the contrary in my progress to Artiwinipeck, where I found, all along that Labrodore coast, no tide at all, a constant current to northward, a precarious ebb and flood of two or three foot, and this entirely under the influence of the winds. This I assert from repeated tryalls and repeated confirmations.

It may be some satisfaction to my reader to know how I could be determined in a matter of this nicety. Know then, in my progress along shore, in attempting to find a harbour near the Point of Portland, at a place I called the Decoy, we touch't the ground, and being too near the sea to expect to ly easy, we lightned our ship eighteen inches, the winds then moderate southerly. As the winds increased, we constantly found the water ebb and flow about nine inches at all hours, for twenty-four hours together, which, as soon as the wind abated, we came off, and in half an hour after it fell calm, not less than twenty inches where we had stuck so long. This every person in the ship and sloop observed as well as my self. I have been the more perticular on this one circumstance, which is of such mighty consequence in determining between those two opinions; for if the eastern tides could reach the western shore of Hudsons Bay, surely the eastern shore would share colaterally, and the times of full sea would hold some proportion, so much nearer their sources : the contrary by this is made manifest.

Thus Middleton, by opposing his own tabular deduction of the tides in Sir Thomas Roe's Welcome, gave Mr. Dobbs cause of triumph ; for a point of the compass or two, in this dispute, is not to be regarded ; for by like parity of reasoning, and like deduction, the correspondent times with correspondent distances, not to say any thing in regard to the heights nor forces (which no man can overlook), the extrems demonstrate the mean. And the mean is undoubtedly the source of that western tide.

From what has been said, it appears highly probable that there is western tide enters Hudsons Bay near Whale Cove, Brook Cobham ; and to the northward of Cape Usquemow, in 61° 10′ N., and 16° 40′ W. longitude from Cape Diggs, we made that cape where it terminates in a point which cuts the tides in eddies, and overfalls, and broken ground, from thirty-five fatham to twenty, in a cast or two ; the ground like black pepper, with yellow shells, and hard ground, and makes not unlike Knights Hill.

Near Whale Cove and Brook Cobham, it is agreed on all hands, their are such sholes of whales and seales, as is no where else to be met with in the known world ; the tides are destracted and strong, flows a great deal of water (*especially with a northerly and westerly wind*), a broken land, and islands innumerable, and consequently long pestered with ice.

I am convinced this has been the main obstacle to that discovery, not the want of a navigable sea. All that I can learn demonstrate this, that they are a congeries of islands, an archipelago ; and lying open every way, loses that head of water so necessary to disincumber them of ice. For where there is a continent, or river only, there would be an accretion of snow uppon the adjacent lands, the disolving of which unlooses the ice, rases a head of water behind it, and so pushes it into the streem ; and there, by the gradual discent of the floods, 'tis thrown out of the tides into open waters, there deposited for the sport of winds, keep the seas cool for the pleasure and recreation of its finny inhabitants and creatures of cold climes.

And even Middleton confirmes me in this conjecture in his letter he intended to prove Wager Streight a fresh-water river, unwarily tells you, the higher he went up that river above Dear Sound, he found the ice, for severall days and severall tryalls, still thicker and closer, forgetting to reflect that, was it a river, it could not possibly happen so, as is demonstrable by the gradual descent of all floods ; a bare deduction will convince any man,[1] viz. :

At Gravesend you have nearly six hours flood and six hours ebb ; at London, five hours flood, and seven hours ebb ; at Richmond, three hours flood, and nine hours ebb ; and at Kingston, two hours flood, and ten hours ebb. So that, you perceive, was the ice broke up in this river, how soon a few tides would clear it of all appearance of ice ; and this rule is incontestable.

On the contrary, where the tides are nearly equally in duration, and wants that head of water, such places will be longer pestred with ice ; and this is our case, as is agreed on by all that ever attempted to penetrate amongst these islands.

It may be necessary to say a word or two on the land and rivers as we find them in that navigation, for the better understanding our geography. Hudson's Streights on both sides is a very high bold land, broken into inlets, and lined with islands innumerable from one end to the other, very steep too everywhere, and the flood setts into those inlets very strong near the shore, and off again uppon the ebb ; this one reason why near the north shore 'tis comonly clear

---

[1] Subsequent examination has proved it to be a river,—or, more correctly speaking, an inlet, into which a small river empties itself,—as reported by Middleton, and not a strait, as conjectured by some : Captain Coats, apparently, among the number.

of ice first, and perhaps it may be so near the south shore ; the snow melting in the declivitys will cause an increment in those out setts.

Mansfield Island, about twenty leagues long, is a low flat island, but rises towards the north end ; is fifteen leagues west from Cape Diggs, and extends S.S.W. nearly to 61° 38' N. ; the south end very low, without bush or braque.

Cape Charles are a cluster of islands ninety miles east from Cape Diggs, the northermost of which is in latitude of 62° 55' ; we found a pritty good harbour on the north side, but on the south side many good harbours ; we took plenty of young ducks, and saw numbers of fowl about them, as is likewise at Mansfield. More of this hereafter, as well as Notingham and Salisbury, and other places not yet taken notice of.

From Cape Pembrock to Cape Southampton is a low barren plain country, nothing distinguishable thereon. You have sounding in sixty fatham regular ground, but nearer then that is broken ground ; the first is a high bold cape, but the latter is a low flatt land ; and I had a hundred and twenty fatham not four miles from that cape ; therefore, forty fatham is near enough in dark wether.

Wager Streight, or River, in 60° 20' N., appears more like a sea, with deap water, high land, a rapid tide, and salt thirty leagues up, and dilates to westward, as was made out to the Committe of the House of Comons.

Whale Cove is moderately high land, broken in islands and inlets, a strong tide, and flows much water ; the flood came from the N.N.W., and the ebb sett amongst them from S.S.E. I was at anchor in eighteen fatham, six miles from the nearest island, in the year 1737.

Seal River, to southward of Cape Usquimow, is a low and barren coast ; the river is choked with islands and sholds, but runs a great way into the country, and with one small land carrige approches a lake or sea, which washes that whole country from whence our northern Indians come down to trade at Churchill River once in two years.

The course of this river, as near as I could make it out from Mack-qua-ta, or Long Day's son, an Indian, is near W.N.W. a hundred and twenty miles, and so leaves a small tract of land between this and Churchill River, where Mr. Norton, master, at Churchill River, appointed that Indian and two other young fellows to observe the motions of the two nations, and so give him notice from time to time what was hatching between them, and so prevented them from continuing the war so distructive to the trade ; and by this means effected and established such a peace as has not been broke since, and now are so united by marrages and kindnessis as give a hopefull prospect for the time to come.

The northern Indians, who by his means only the company became acquainted with, ordered him in the year to travill into their country, and reside amongst them for a considerable time, in order to draw them down to trade, and make what observations he could ; but as he was very young and unqualified for any great matter, I did not find anything remained on his memory, but the danger and terrour he underwent; but to the day of his death he had an affectionate kindness for that people.

These northern Indians are an exact compound between the Usquemows and western Indians ; are robust and wild ; not so delicate as the western Indians ; negligent of their persons to the last degree; very fond of iron and iron tolls of all sorts ; and so indifferent about rain and sunshine or tempestious weather, as if they had lost all degrees of sense. For my own part, I saw a gang of them once at Churchill River, whom I thought so savage and brutal, that I litle expected anything rational from them. And yet the leader of those Indians asked us many pertinant questions ; very inquisitive into our manner of life ; from whence we brought those goods ? where we got our iron ? went all over the ship ;

examined our anchors, cables, and in short everything he saw; the compass he took for a toy, and all we could do or say about it made him laugh.

The iron, he said, his countrymen valued most; and our guns they liked very well; but the want of powder and shot induced them to cut them up for knives and chizzells; so that, on the whole, he thought nothing we brought was worth their trouble only the wrought iron.

In this resembles the Usquemows; but contrary to them they generally dress their victuals, live in tents, not in caves as those do, live more on inland food, as wolves, deer, and other wild creatures; not as those, on whale's oyl and blubbers, and other train; they are not so megre, thin, and raw boned, as the western Indians; nor so bloated, squatt, and sallow, as the Usquemows. So, as I before said, they are a compound of both, and their life and manners demonstrate this.

To the southward of Seel River our western Indians are dispersed in tribes and familys, not under any monarchical goverment, but truely patriarchical, as far as I can observe; and there youth are as absolutely under the tuition and disposal of the old men as in the most arbitrary country in the world; this is most certainly that freedom of nature and independency which the antient poets dreamed of, but is nowhere to be found in the known world but amongst these savages; their obedience is not servile, but love and emulation; and their eldest sons succeed in the preeminence of his family.

There are many barbarious customs amongst them; too tedious, and in some measure foreign to my subject, the geography of that countrye.

It will be necessary, before I quitt these parts, to set down my own sentiments and that of others, in regard to the Usquemows, the naturall inhabitants of all the northern borders of Hudson's Bay and Streights, which swarms with

robust hardy fellows fitt for the severest exercise, and indeed
with such dispositions, as if God's providence in fullness of
time had prepared them to receive the yoke of civility. And
I do assert of my own knowledge, that these people are
nothing near so savage as is represented by our early voyagers, and that there confidence is in their innocence, not in
their numbers, which I have often experienced when one or
two has put themselves into my hand without reserve or
caution.

I am of opinion with others, that if the company had
thought it their interest (and if their were not political reasons to the contrary), that discovery had been determined
long before this time, and those swarms of God's people
made usefull in trade and reclaimed from horrid idolitry.

There is one difficulty occurs in reducing this numerous
people to civility, and that is their way of life and dyett,
which makes extreemly so for Europeans to setle amongst
them; the want of fuel makes it necessary to eat raw meat.
But, notwithstanding, if the company would give leave to
others, or do it themselves, to shelter in the woody parts of
the bay, and so return annually into those parts amongst
the Usquemows, and continue all the summer months for
a year or two, and by degrees penitrate to westward;—I
say a fishery more beneficial than the furr trade might, in
seven years time, be rased amongst that people, and those
tribes made usefull to us, and acquire salvation to themselves; but if, in this progress, a passage should be found to
the South Sea, it would open to us such a scene of treasure
and honour, as no nation of the world (save one) ever enjoyed
before.

I am satisfied the time is near at hand that this great work
is to be undertaken, by whom I cannot forsee. The Company is unpardonable in leaving such swarms of Gods people
in the hands of the devill, unattempted, as well as the other
Indians in generall, a docile, inoffensive, good-natured,

humane people, ofring and bowing to the yoke, yet shame-
fully neglected, not to give it a harder name ; as if gorging
ourselves with superfluitys was the ultimate condition of this
life, and as for that in another life, we were neither much
concerned for them, nor our selves.

These are the methods I think most probable to succeed,
and accomplish this great work, and by degrees reconcile
them to our manner of life and accustome ourselves to theirs,
and gradually advance this laudable business untill it is
completed.

For to the eternal shame of those people, all the litle
attempts made for the Company were rather to amuse than
effect this business ; and the time appointed, and the persons
employed, so unequal to the task, as posterity will blush to
observe[1] how sordid and selfish this generation has been.

Churchill River, in latitude 59° 00′ N., and 95° 00′ west
longitude from London (in Indian, Manato-e-sepe, a sea-like
river), has an entrance from ten to seven fathom water deep,
and steep on both sides, but rocky, and a most violent tide
of ebb, which is owing to the form of that river, which
expands itself from an entrance of about a third of a mile
from Cape Mary to Usquemow Point ; within from Buttons
Rock to the opposite shore, is five mile over.

Uppon Usquemow Point the Company have erected a
stone fort of a quadrangular figure, which is sufficient to
defend the enterence into this river. Three miles up, you
have water for any ship, but higher up 'tis full of sholds and

---

[1] Posterity may well blush, when they read the following remarks
of Sir Edward Parry in his second voyage :—" Upon the whole, it was
impossible for us not to receive a very unfavourable impression of the
general behaviour and moral character of the natives of this part of
Hudson's Strait (the Savage Islands), who seem to have acquired, by an
annual intercourse with our ships for nearly a hundred years, many of
the vices which unhappily attend a first intercourse with the civilized
world, without having imbibed any of the virtues or refinements which
adorn and render it happy."

flatts, and very stoney. Above Musketa Point is a fall of water, which terminates the navigation of this river to any other than very small boats and canoes, who track up this ridge of stones, where our people are plagued in getting down their rafts of timber for fire wood and other uses, which they float down many miles, for all below is cleared and cut down some years ago. About twenty miles above that ridge is a colaterall branch falls into this river, called Litle Churchill, where is caught the finest jack in the world. There titimegg is a fish not unlike our largest white herrings, very good food, and in great plenty in the fall of the year; but below, near the mouth of this river, is. such sholes of salmon trout, as they sometimes salt as much as half victual the factorye. White Whale is here in abundance, spring and fall, and seels, the natural and heriditary enemy of that fish: there are muscles, and a sort of sprey, thrown ashore in stormy weather, not much unlike our spratts; but no perch nor sturgoon, as in the other rivers.

This river runs in from Usquemow Point, near north and south, ten mile to Muskeeta Point, near the fall, and then winds round to westward, and runs upwards of two hundred miles, where, with a small carrage, they arrive on the shore of the great lake, Winipeggon.

The Indians have many very expressive terms in their language. This river, from its great breadth and length, is called Manato-e-sepe, a sea-like river; this lake is caled Winipeggon-e-sepe, or the great sea, is but litle inferiour to Hudsons Bay for breadth, and length, and depth of water;[1] and islands and woods scattered everywhere; and communicates with other lakes to southward, more of which hereafter; but also extends it self nearly N.W. to an indetermined distance, from the north western shores of which I judge our Miscota Indians come to Churchill River to trade

---

This is, of course, a great error, Lake Winnipeg not being one-third of the length, nor an eighth part of the width of Hudson's Bay.

every other year; but wether they come thro the northern Indian country, or the Nadowissis country (another nation of Indians, situated on the western banks of Winipeggon), who trade at Yorkfort once in two year, our interpriters are not clear in. These Miscota Indians tell us some visionary storeys of ships and men of a different make and complection frequenting there shores, for they are positive this lake is open to westward; and do attempt to discribe their gilded beeks, and sails, and other matters, both tedious and tiresome, without we had better grounds; since our acquaintance with these three sorts of people are but of a late date; and whether it was curiosity or necessity that brought them first to our settlements, they seem to despise many things that the other Indians are very fond of.

This lake, or sea, Winipeggon, so far we are pretty certain, is not above a hundred and seventy miles to westward of Churchill River, and that the southern extremity is in latitude of 59° N.; so that the position of this inland sea readily accounts for those extrodinary tides which are observable all along the western coasts of Hudsons Bay, with northerly and westerly winds; and this is so notorious and remarkable, as can hardly escape the notice of the most stupid fellow that ever wintered at Churchill River.

At Yorkfort, in Hays River, the angular inclination of that coast, took in those forcible tides in their course from the north, which might incline us to think it was raised by that possition near that place. But at Churchill those winds blow from the land, and should flatt the tides, not raise them, if propogated from the eastward.

And that the Winipeggon does communicate with Hudsons Bay[1] to the northward of Cape Usquemow, is so generally known and understood by almost every person who have

---

[1] Lake Winnipeg empties itself at its northern extremity into a river, which flowing through a chain of small lakes discharges itself into Hudson's Bay at Port Nelson.

resided there any time, that I am at a loss to account for the absurdity of some persons conduct. To northward of that cape are islands innumerable; but the ice, the tides, and other embarrissments not fit to perticularize in this place, always prevented our people from pushing in there, notwithstanding the many incentives before taken notice of.

The trade at Churchill has rose from 8000 skins to 18,000, bever and woolves chiefly, and but a few martins; and it may be increased, and it will increase, by time, to 40,000, if their was not political reasons to the contrary. However, our stone fort will be a fine security for the trade at that place.

In coasting along to Cape Churchill, eight leagues from Usquemow Point, you meet the sholes of Knight's Hill, a remarkable spot of earth, deposited in a fenn, to caution seamen of those dangers near it, whose banks and ridges run of to sea six mile; by another note he says eight miles, and that nine fathom is too near them day and night; and so on to the cape, about six leagues farther to eastward, to sail round which come no nearer than ten fathom. And then a south by east course to 57° 40′ latitude, in fifteen to twenty fathom, you come to Port Nelsons sholes; in crossing a spitt which shoots from them, with a S.S.E. course, you come into seven fatham and hard ground, and so into fifteen fatham soft; and so continue that course from fifteen fatham soft, untill you gradually sholding into seven fatham hard, there you come to anchor and wate the tide, to go over the flatt to Hay's River.

The shore from Cape Tatnam to Marsh Point lyes east by north, and west by south. By edging on the flatts into three fatham, you rase the factory and Marsh Point, or see the becon in Five Fathom Hole. You will carry fifteen foot at an ordinary tide, in the fair way, when the factory bears S.W. by W. and beacon W.S.W., good nine mile over that flatt into Five Fathom Hole, a bason three quarters of a mile in diameter. Two mile higher up is a hole three fatham deep, sufficient for one ship. The river, up three miles to the factory, dry's almost every tide.

Note, " the difference of longitude from Churchill River, at Usquemow Point, to Five Fatham Hole in Hay's River, is 2° 20′ E.; but to come round Port Nelson shoalds, in 57° 40′ N., you must go 2° 35′ E.; the Hole is in latitude 57° 10′ N. You observe, in coasting, you should not go without twenty or twenty-two fatham, least you should fall in with the shoalds of Cape Tatnam, nor nearer than fifteen fatham, least you be embarrised with the shoalds of Port Nelson."

York Fort, in Hay's River, has the most principle trade in that country, where the two rivers brings down such swarms of natives annually, as is nowhere else in that country. Port Nelson is by much the most navigable for ships, and near half the trade come down that river; but 'tis so full of sharps and falls, that most of our Indians chuse Hay's River, and 'tis more secure, and better for the Company, guarded by those flatts and shallows against the attempts of an enemy by sea, the only way to come at this settlement. As to the extent of these two rivers, they run up seventy miles nearly parrelel to one another, between the south and west, and there unite, forming that island the settlement is made uppon; from thence it runs into some morassis and beaver grounds, and has its source in an infinity of litle lakes, which dilate themselves in rivulets into the Lake Nimipigon,[1] which stretches nearly N.W. and S.E. above sixty leagues in length, and in breadth nearly forty leagues, from 53° of latitude to 56°, in form of a philbert, where enters a streight seventy-five leagues in length from the N.N.W. out of the Winipeggon-e-sepe, before explained, the eastern border of which is in 100° W. longitude from London.

This Lake Nimipeggon has many islands covered with

[1] Lake Winnipegoos.

wood, and the borders are replenished with dear, and all
sorts of beasts, and men; the lake abounds with fish, titimegg (at the proper seasons in prodigious quantities, which
the Indians smoak and dry for winter food), perch, and
mathii, and sturgoon very large, and fine eating: all these
different species of fish come down our rivers into Hudson's
Bay at some seasons of the year, and are caught by our
people—sturgeon, mathii, and charming perch as big as a
small cod, and titimegg, at our southern settlements; jack,
salmon, and titimegg, at our northern settlements. Our
trading Indians from all those countrys assert that the Winipeggon is filled with salt water very deep, with seals and
whales and other sorts of fish in abundance.

The western borders of this Lake Winipeggon is inhabited
by the Nadouissis; more to southward is the Sinipoots; to
southward of them is the Poots and Stone Indians; farther
south is the Cristians; and to southward of them is the
Sturgoon Indians.

The northern borders of that great lake is occupied by
the Miscota and northern Indians, who partake so much of
the features and complection of the Usquemows, that I am
perswaded they are near neighbours to one another.

But those tribes to westward of the lake extend to an
indetermined distance. Wither Mr. Kelsey was amongst
those western Indians when he traviled to cultivate the company trade, or the more southerly Indians, I am not well
informed; but this is certain, that the Poots, Senepoots, and
Stone Indians, have frequented York Fort many years; the
Nadouissis, Christians, and Sturgoon Indians, is of a later
date; the Miscota are a nation we have had a much shorter
acquaintance with; and their unequal war with the Nadowissis, a powerfull and warlike people, inspired them with
motives to seek out fire-arms, which the northern Indians,
their kindred and frinds, first brought them to Churchill
River.

All these tribes and nations are situated on the western sides of those lakes, from latitude 61° to 47°, to westward of the Superior Lake, and the streights from lake to lake, and do generally come down every year, or once in two years, to trade at York Fort.

Those countrys that ly between Hudsons Bay on the east, and those great lakes on the west, are occupied by a mixed moungril people of many tribes, as great and litle Winipeggons; their very names tells us where they come from, when the lakes are well fixed.  The Cristians, I must acknowledge, are an unmixed people; I have seen them as fair as the Europeans, and nothing like the other Indians, but in their manner of life.  The Pike Indians, Owashoes, and Eagle Eyes, do all go down to Albany; the great and litle Tabitabies, Piscotagemies, and Miscosinks, do frequent Moose River; all the rest of the wandring tribes are those we call Home Indians, or from those lakes.  It is amongst these tribes that the French wood-runners make such inroads on our borders; nor is it in the power of man to prevent it growing worse and worse, without we could fall on a way to send our people amongst the Indians, to live and hunt, and marry and mix, and encounter and drive those pedlers back into their own lakes.

For I dont find those wood-runners ever made any progress much to northward of the Superior Lake; and some of the branches on the eastern side, and those to westward, seem always to have been strangers to them, perhaps owing to the intestine warrs and divisions amongst those different tribes.

These lakes so defined occupies the greatest part of that inland country.  And thus has those idle, indolent, happy wanderers in their paradise, freed from the curse of all civilized countrys, ambition and want, the pleasure and benefit of rambling into far distant countrys, without the hazard of being surprized by more savage Europeans, in

6

contentment and ease of mind, in lazy luxery, without per-
turbation or misgiving for want.

On the contrary, are so hospitaly inclined, that if by
chance they meet any sterved Indians, or familys of sterved
Indians, they immediately share fate with them, and cannot,
nor will not, enjoy a morsal untill those are provided for,
not scantily, but in the same measure and manner with himself.  I knew an instance of this, of two familys of Indians
at Churchill, in the year 1742 or 1743, one whose name in
English was Warrior, the other Atequenow.  The Warrior
meets him in the barren plain a starving for want, and himself well stock't with provissions, he gave him a small supply,
and haistned into the hunting grounds, and lift poor Atequenow to strugle with famine in a barren plain : finally,
they dyed, and eat one another, and so the whole family was
cut off, all but two vigorous children, who in great extremity
reach't that factory.  Some time after, the Warrior comes
down to trade, the other Indians upbraids him ; amongst
other expressions, tells him he was as savage and greedy as
the French or English ; he retires immediately into his tent,
covers his head, and dyes in a few hours after.

This is matter of fact ; and altho' I was not an eye-witness
when the Warrior dy'd, I was at Churchill a few days after,
when his family was in the utmost confusion about it.

Here's humanity ! here's virtue in perfection ! this is what
the antients dreamed of ; but is nowhere in the known world
to be found but amongst these savages.

You will say, my sons, that a people so happy in almost
every circumstance of life, should have multiply'd and increased much faster then it appears they have.  I answer,
their fugitive rambling life from place to place, is destruc-
tive to their younger chilldren ; for 'tis certain their women
bring forth their chilldren much easier and without injury
than ours do ; and sometimes this indolent security over-
takes them in those barren plains,— and so hungar, the

only distemper that kills an Indian, dispatches a whole family.

The Indians shew us their wisdom on divers occasions, and in none more than in their choice of names of creatures and places, which always imply something of their natures and qualitys ; which I could evince by too instances: thus, Winipeggon is a larger lake or sea, Nimipeggon is a lesser lake or sea ; Awteck Winnepeeggon, a place where deer abounds ; our rivers Manato-e-sepe, a sea-like river, a sea-like lake, and a thousand more such significant terms ; islands the same, Agomisco, Sick, where deer herds ; the like of fish and fowl.

Ticko-omo, a deer haunt ; Metesina, a place of refreshment ; Kato-ecan, a fine hunting ground ; Komo-so-ta-co, a place where deer herds ; Coapachi-oun-e-seepe,[1] a fresh-water river ; Qua-qua-chich-i-uan, it swallows quickly our gulph hazard ; Mischigitu-e-seepe, a river without bounds, our Great White Whale River, *cum multis aliis*. This inteligent way of fitting names informs them at once what may be expected in those places, and is so extrodinary usefull to posterity, and renders our arbritary distinctions quite contemptable.

And the better our governours and people have made themselves acquainted with these people, they have always had a stronger impression of their judgement and wisdom.

Those three larger lakes, and a multitude of lesser lakes, nearly parellel and equidistant from Hudsons Bay, affords by their branches an easy communication with the rivers and creeks of Hudsons Bay, by the vast falls of snow which makes such floods and flows of water as greatly facilitate that roving wandring disposition of this idle, indolent, happy people ; and we are pritty certain all or most of those Indians

---

[1] The same significant terms are still adopted by the natives : for instance, the Thleweechodezeth, or Great Fish River, discovered by Sir George Back.

on this side those lakes come down to trade annually, and those Indians to westward of those lakes every other year, to one or other of our setlements; the wood-runners endeavour to way lay them, and sometimes come in for a chasing part, especially amongst the mungril tribes; but those western Indians in national tribes are such as the pedlers are shy of meeting with.

From the Point of Marsh at the mouth of Port Nelson River up to Flambrough Head, a bluff high land on the north-west side, is twenty-eight miles, and navigable for any ship, where you meet with a cluster of islands and a fall which terminates that navigation; not but small boats and canoes get over with some difficulty, and have a fine chanile for many miles above (and I have heard that a ship might get over this fall if she waited some high raging tides in the fall of the year); it is about twelve miles wide at the Point of Marsh, and so inclines gradually to about four miles in breadth against that headland. At eight miles distance is Hay's River; above the factory is a creek, against which in Port Nelson is another, which in a manner meet, where the natives in bad wether unload their canoes, and come over into Hay's River, rather than go round the Point of Marsh: this pass would be of great consequence if ever the Company come to be rival'd in that trade. However, the Company has delay'd to secure this place sooner; their orders was sent in the year 1749, to erect a fortification on that side to secure that pass and shut up that river.

In sailing into that river, take your soundings from the south shore, in five to three fatham, to avoid falling into broken ground to northward, which is very stud too; but you have flatt and fair soundings on the south side. With this precaution you may, in dark wether, sail safely into Port Nelson, six or eight mile up course, nearly S.W. by S. In this noble, capacious river, the antient worthys took shelter, and immagined none other would answer so well for

the business of trade and for a comfortable residence, and a
settlement was made ; but soon after was removed where it
now stands, at the concurrent request of all the natives, for
the reasons before mentioned.  This river has a most extrodinary flux, owing to those unbounded flatts ; and the fall
produces a violent reflux, which keeps the mouth of this
extrodinary river always open in winter, whence proceeds
those pernicious frost-mist's, which affects the eyes and lungs
of our people in a most deplorable manner ; for which
nothing is so effectual as bleeding and sweating, if worse,
blistering ; but the continuation and repetition of these
remidy's impaires our peoples health so much, that very few
ever escaped this dreadfull calamity.  This is attended with
so exquisit a pain that it is never mentioned by any who
ever were afflicted with it but with terrour.  The Indians
always bleed and sweet with the steam of warm water : this
remidy, altho slower, I am of opinion do less wound the fine
capillaries of the lungs, where the seat of this malady do
principly ly ; and if the faculty would excuse me, I could
assine a reason why those mists are so hurtfull in that part.
This steam arises from a mixture of salt and fresh water,
which is immediately congealed into ice, very hard ; so
wafted into the lungs, into those fine capillaries, without
being disolved.  This sudden and violent effect is made
before nature can reconcile her self to so prodigious an
extream : hence those convulsions and straitnings that give
that exquisite pain.

From the mouth of Port Nelson to Cape Tatnam is near
twenty leagues distance, E.N.E., by true chart, along a flatt
shore, from five to ten fatham deep, in a channile about six
leagues broad, over to Port Nelson shoalds.  The cape is
flatt off a great way, to 57° 35', variation, 17° N.westerly in
the 1740, where the coast winds away E.S.E. ; but flatt and
sandy, and the coast very low but woody ; twelve miles along
shore you meet the east and west Pens, two litle woody

islands. And in latitude 56° 00′ is a fine river, caled Severn, which dilates itself into far distant countrys, communicates with all those lakes, and affords, by its branches, an easy enterence into all the other rivers : hence the Indians go indifferently to Albany, to Hays, and Port Nelson. About forty years ago, the Company had a setlement on this river, and the trade was considerable ; but uppon the recovery of York Fort by the peace of Utrecht, the Company throwed it up as not worth the expence, and the trade is divided between Albany and that place. The mouth of this river is said to be shoald ; but the bar is not near so broad as at Hays River. This coast and river is cover'd with wood every where, and a pritty clean shore without ten or twelve fatham.

From Severn River to Cape Henrietta Maria, in latitude 55° 10′ N., the course is E.S.E. ; to westward of which, in 55° 30′, near Cape Look-out, is some broken ground, banks, and ridges, a great way off, come no nearer than seventeen fatham ; the land, very low and fenny, appears here and there in tufts of trees.

To southward of the Cape, the land run S.S.E. very low, but clean, even soundings, with wood in some places. The shore is flatt a good way of. S.E. from Cape Henrietta Maria, seventeen leagues distance, is a cluster of barren islands, four larger in number, and many lesser, from 54° 40′ to 54° 28′, caled the Bear Islands, in thirty fatham water, cliffy, and not so low as the main, higher than the hull of a ship. Five leagues east from the south Bear, is a rock one mile in circumference, caled the Cubb.

In coasting down James Bay, you are to observe to keep from ten or twelve fatham into twenty-two fatham, to avoid the islands to eastward ; and so on, S. by E., into 53° 30′, you come to the west end of Agomisco, and so regard those depths into 53° 00′, where you come to the north-east corner of that great island, where you fall into broken ground and deep water, twenty-five or thirty fatham in a cast or two.

East, seven leagues from this point, are four islands, named Weston's Isles; E.N.E. nine leagues, are two Twins of a moderate bigness, and barren, cliffy land, with some scatered wood here and there. E.S.E. fourteen leagues, is fine bold island, caled Soloman's Temple ; and so, on a chain is some scattered islands, nearly S.S.E., to Trodileys, to Charlton Danbys and Caries, in 52° 10'; to eastward of those are numberless nameless islands. N.B.—There is a rock, S.W., sixteen miles from the South Bear, in latitude 54° 20' N., which I named Floatars Wash, from an accident of that man, who was drowned there.

From the north-east corner of Agomisco, S.S.E. thirty-two miles, in latitude 52° 32' N., is a dry bank called the Gaskitt. 'Tis about two mile long, S.S.W. and N.N.E., and drys half a mile ; you have fifteen fatham close to eastward of it, and five, six, seven fatham to westward. I am of opinion there is a wide, open channile to westward of it; 'tis thirty-two miles to eastward of Albany Road ; 'tis fifty-seven miles to eastward of the South Bear, and that island is twenty-five miles to westward of the North Sand Head in Albany River ; 'tis fifty-eight miles N. by E. from Moose River Road, and twenty-one miles W.S.W. from Trodiley Island.

From the Gaskitt, fifty-eight miles S. by W., you come to Moose River Road ; eight mile north from Sand Heads, North Point, W.N.W., six mile, in latitude 51° 34' N., where you wate for the tide to go into that wide-mouthed river, which is not less than twelve miles over, from the North Point to the opposite shore, which opens with three channiles; but the north and eastern are so choked with banks and shoalds, and there is no using those ; the midle chanile will admit of a ship of twelve foot. Observing the tide over a bar one mile broad, and one mile within the Sand Heads, is a litle place affords water for a ship to ly afloat, caled the Lower Ship Hole, to distinguish it from another four mile above Sand Heads, caled Ship Hole, in three fatham, low water, where we moor and do our business. Eight mile below the factory on Robersons Islands, from Midlebrough, another island runs a shoald within half a mile of the ship, which cuts the river, and prevents the ship going to the factory, which has water plenty all above that place. In this river you have many islands, all covered with wood, as is the sides everywhere, except here and there 'tis interspersed with Savannahs. The wood is spruce, pine, popler, juniper, and some burch, shrubbs of many sort, covered with variety of berrys, as huckle-berrys, blew-berrys, cranberrys, juniper-berrys, a fine yellow berry caled pithogatomines, straw-berrys, and bramble-berrys. This great variety, intermixed with those evergreens, afford a most delightfull prospect; and, indeed, Moose River is the garden of Hudsons Bay.

Notwithstanding, I know not by what ill-fated policy this settlement has, ever since its settlement in the year 1732, struggled with great difficulty in regard to country provisions.

The Indians in this neighbourhood, by their longer inter-course with the English and French, are more sociable, more civell, and a better genious for trade, more humane, and not so savage, as in the northern parts of the bay, and require more address and management to make them usefull to the settlement, which, I doubt, has been so much neglected, and which has been a great injury to this settlement and trade hitherto; for 'tis as well replenished with fish, and fowl, and deer, and other cretures, as any of the other settlements, and rabbits in greater abundance. 'Tis true the marshes are wider, and the deluges are more violent, which root up and sweep of whole plains, and plow up that sort of grass the fowl are so fond of, near the borders of this river; but as these are to be had uppon as easy terms as at any other settlement, by going a litle way out of the verge of these deluges. Surely 'tis a monstrous oversight; and the Indians are so sensible of this, that they have treated our people with a proportionable contempt; and this appeared so plain to one of our modern governours, who had but a very litle correspondence with these people, and observing the miscarrages of those before, he proposed, executed, and accomplished, in one season, a greater supply of provisions than ever was known at that setlement, by the aid and advice of these very people. This shows what may be done, and likewise, what has been neglected, left undone!

About eight miles above the factory is a cluster of islands, near which is a fall of the river, where boats and canoos are track't up, where the river is collected into a narrower compass, and deape water, and so collected extends itself into distant countrys, as far as latitude 47° 00', but is divided into two main branches: the greater runs S.W., and terminates in the great Tabitabi Lake; the other branch runs south, and ends the lesser Tabittabi. These two lakes affords, by their branches, an easy comunication with the lakes of Canada, Piscataggama on the west, and Camasinck on the east; and the trade was considerably inlarged by the address of the aforesaid person, but was removed for reasons best known to the Company. Moose River is called, in Indian, Moose-e-sepee, from the abundance of those deer; also Nimmow-e-sepee, from the abundance of sturgeon in itt. The countrys bordering on this river is said to be very fertile, and capible of any culture; and the summer season not so short, nor the winter so severe, as in other parts of the bay; and abounds with jack, perch, mathyi, titimegg, and sturgeon, the finest and largest I ever saw, which these Indians smoak and dry at proper seasons. And you but seldom hear of any starved Indians hereabout; wether 'tis owing to fewer barren grounds, or to a greater plenty of provision every where, I leave it to more proper judges; and I am told that rabbits may be had in quantitys always.

From the outer bouy of this river, eight miles E. by S. from the North Point to Albany Road, is sixty miles by computation, six mile to the bluff, twenty-one miles more to

7

Wapisco, eighteen more to Cockispenny, and twenty-four miles more to the buy, in the fair way going into that river, N.N.W. ½ W., W.W. by N., and N.W. by W., in five fatham, twenty-one miles east from the fort on Bailey's Island, eight miles within the north Sand Head, and thirty-two miles W. by S. from the Gaskitt, in latitude 52° 22′ N., by a fine observation, and where a south moon makes full sea, rises uninfluenced about eight foot water, and the variation is 16° north-westerly.

The river is full of shoalds at the mouth, and a vessel of ten foot may go to the factory very safely ; but the buisness is now done by a sloop, and no ship has been in this river this twenty-five years, for reasons best known to the Company ; for sure I am you seldom escape a gale in that wild road, esspecially in the fall, as put all at stake ; the ground is a light oaz, and very bad anchorage. This river extends its self nearly W.S.W. about three hundred miles, and by a small carrage into Mitchipekitan, hold on a navigable course into the Superior Lake in latitude 50° 00′, from whence the French encroach into the Companys borders, and endeavour to allure our Indians to trade with them ; and, the better to succeed therein, erected a setlement on this river, within a hundred and twenty miles of Albany Fort, and resided there a considerable time, and did this setlement a great deal of damage ; but by some mismanagement amongst themself, it was deserted, and the Company, in the year 1741, erected a block-house near that place, which commands the two branches of that river : since which no French Indian has resided on that river, altho we constantly hear of their roving amongst the scattered tribes, and with their guegaws and nicknacks have had, by times, a great influence over this good-natured indolent people. But those been practised so often uppon them, that the jest is worn out, and that *meum* and *tuum* is the word by which only the Company has the ascendent, not only in a greater choice of goods, but better pennorths; which, as I observed before, these Indians are more polite, and are most accustomed to trade.

This river, after you are within the shallows, is a fine navigable river, many miles up, and the sharps and falls are fewer than in most rivers in the country. The western branch, one hundred miles up, do verge on the heads of Severn and Port Nelson : hence the Indians descend indifferently into all our rivers, which afford our people so easy a comunication and inteligence, that none of the wood-runners can haunt that wide-extended country but in a very short time all our governours may know it, and take their measures accordingly. As we know their wants, and know their practises, the neglect of this wise policy will be always an injury to the Company.

The Superior Lake is four degrees from north to south, and is 9° 00′ of longitude from east to west, between 84° and 93° west from London. 'Tis caled Superior, or Upper Lake, by the Europeans; I suppose, from the descent of the waters falling into the Hurons and Illinease, and other lakes of Canada, at the streight of St. Maria, where is a fall caled Sauteures; or as being the ultimate progress of the French, for the reason I mentioned.

On the northern borders of this lake are many islands, which the French geographers have confounded with other names than the first discoverers gave them, and hold forth to us the expediency of retaining as many of the Indian names as we can get, to make our geography inteligible ! The only island I shall take notice of, Lahonten cales Minong, near which enters a streight seventy leagues from the N.W., long which passis through the Pike Indian country into the Nimi-peggon-e-sepee before discribed.

James Bay is an arm of Hudsons Bay, extending from Cape Henrietta Maria, in 55° 10′, to Moose River, in 51° 34′, and is, in breadth, fifty-four leagues from east to west, inclining, as you sail, to southward, and has many embarrissments, which you are carefully to attend too.

Point Look-out lyes twenty leagues to westward of Cape Henrietta Maria, in latitude 56° 00′; to eastward of which, uppon an E.S.E. course, lyes many a bank and shoald, some of whom I have seen dry in seven, eight, and ten fatham water ; and therefore, to avoid which, seventeen or twenty fatham is near enough, and then you have soft, even ground ; the banks are hard, stoney ground.

If you are entangled in ice here, you run great hazard, for the tides are so distracted amongst these banks, that it will require your utmost address to secure your ship: when clear, the tide setts east and west.

As you come towards Cape Henrietta Maria, you will find your soundings more even and flatt ; a long way of, a more wheyish colour, which, as you sail to eastward, and deapen your water, it grows blacker and blacker, untill it becomes of a deap galle colour ; and soft ground in twenty or twenty-five fathom from broken ground and shoald water in a litle distance.

You may then steer south, or nearly so, into fifteen fatham. Regard the colour of your water, which, when you shoalden into less, your water turns quickly wheaish ; and I can tell my depth of water nearly by this observation.

In these depths, from fifteen to twenty-four fatham, you sail very safely, taking your soundings from the shore.  If you go to eastward into deeper water, you meet many embarrissments ; and more to westward, is to near the Bear Islands, in latitude 54° 38′, to 54° 28′, four larger and many lesser, with sundry reefs of rocks, which would hook you in, if you are not very cautious, in a fog, or dark night.

Near the same latitude, on the west main, is a bluff of wood, caled Point Mourning, from buriing one of Captain James men there.  The land to northward of this, and westward of the cape, is all a low fenny unbounded marsh,

not to be seen but in very fine weather, so that your lead is
your principle guide.

Seventeen mile S.W. from the South Bear, in the fair way,
is a rock, dry at half tide, a quarter of a mile long, I named
Floaters Wash, in twenty-five fatham, close too on all sides ;
and fifteen miles due east from the said South Bear, is a rock
as high as the hull of a ship, one mile in circumference,
caled the Cubb, in thirty-five fatham. There is a bank runs
fifteen leagues from the Cubb towards the North Twinn,
with ten, twelve, fourteen, when to the westward you have
twenty-two fatham soft ground and black water ; therefore,
in dark and foggy weather, we hold it safest to coast it up
along the west main from fifteen to twenty fatham, which
prevents your falling in with those embarrissment, and keeps
you clear of Litle Agomisco on the west main.

In latitude 53° 40′, where you may shoulden into eight or
nine fatham, and is even flatt ground a great way off, and
haul of to eastward about E.S.E. in those depths, till you
have broken ground, and in a cast or two, thirty or thirty
five fatham near the north-east point of Agomisco.

From hence you steer S.E. by S. thirty-two miles in 25,
22, 18, 22, 20. You will come to a dry bank a quarter of
a mile long, but the reefs from it may be two mile, N.N.E.
and S.S.W., caled the Gaskitt ; between this and Agomisco
is a pretty good chanile, but disused on account of the broken
ground near Agomisco ; the latitude of this bank, by a fine
observation, is 52° 32′, and lyes fourteen miles to eastward
of the north-east horn or point of Agomisco.

In sailing near the south and eastern part of Agomisco,
you must take care of your tides, which setts nearly N.E.
and S.W., and the tide of ebb runs pritty briskly, and will
sett you eastward amongst the islands, which is not to be
prevented but by keeping your lead strickly fifteen or
twenty fathams, and black water will free you from many
apprehensions.

After you pass the Gaskitt, you come to a ridge of hard
ground, in ten, eleven, nine fatham, from which S.S.W. brings
you into fourteen, thirteen, fifteen fatham soft ground, which
is the most you must expect to southward of the Gaskitt;
thirty-two mile west from this ridge is Albany Road, in five
fatham, and latitude 52° 20′, when the fort in the river is
west from you twenty-one mile, where a south moon makes
full sea, 16° north-westerly variation; fifty-eight miles south
from the Gaskitt, you come into Moose River Road, in five
fatham, soft but good anchor ground, E. by S.; seven miles
from the North Point, the North Bluff, in going into Moose
River, the coast from Albany to Moose River, nearer than
five fatham, is all banks and broken ground, the land is low
and cover'd with woods, and winds like a bow; south from
the Northsand Head in Albany River, are the Canuce
Creeks; twelve miles more easterly is Natititia; four miles
farther is Nomansland; a broken point shoots of some distance, S.E. by E., twenty-four miles from Albany Road,
carrys you near this point, in six fatham, near enough;
Kokeishpenny is a litle island four miles more easterly,
where the coast winds about S.E. by S.; fifteen miles bring
you to Wapisco, another little island, which makes a bay,
and affords anchor ground with westerly winds; from this to
the North Point is eighteen miles, S. by E., in not less than
five fatham, when the point bears S.W. to W.S.W., you are
then uppon the broken ground, and may run a ground if
you are not very carefull of your lead; this is the rule for
dark and hazy weather, but when it is fair and clear, and
the land appears true, you may keep in six or seven fatham,
and the North Point will direct you into Moose River Road;
and 'tis to be noted, all the land is cover'd with trees, with
some litle intervals, which makes it apear so bold as to be
seen into ten fatham from the deck.

To eastward of that river's mouth towards Indian Head,
the tufts and hummacks appear over that fenny shore here

and there, but so shallow, there is no coming nigh it, till
you come near that head, which lys E.S.E. thirty-two miles
from the North Point, in latitude 51° 30, from thence to
Point Comfort, E. by N. twenty-seven miles, and so over to
Mount Shaddock, E.N.E. twenty-seven miles, is the true
distance from the west to the east main.

To eastward of Indian Head is a deep bay, which insinu-
ates itself into 51° 10′, and expands itsself to eastward
twenty-six miles, at the bottam of which is two larger and
one lesser creeks or rivers, on the western and southern side
of this bay, Seal more northerly, and Onahanna River more
sotherly, which comes from Theketowesakee Masshishcock,
a good place to shoot geese in; more to eastward in this
great bay is another river caled Pisquamisquow; these
rivers or creeks verge on Nodoway River, whence the French
Indians in all their attempts on our settlements, the whole
coasts flatt off.

Point Comfort is a peninsula, from whence the coast
declines to southward into those bays, to westward and eastward into the mouth of Nodoway River, near the entrance
of which is a fine creek caled Thompson's, who, it is said,
he wintered his vessel there; 'tis to be noted, our first
voyagers had such dreadfull apprehensions of the deluges in
all our principle rivers, that they often grapled with great
inconveniencys of another kind; but now 'tis otherwise, and
our people make no difficulty of, and shelter our ships and
sloops everywhere.

This great river, caled by the natives Notowaes, or Uta-
wawas Autáwas, with a large mouth, opens itsself a passage
nearly S. and S.S.E. to a great distances, and falls into the
Lakes of Saguina and Tadussock, on the eastern verge of
the Superior Lake, whence a small distance into Canada
without a carrage; those Lakes of Saguina, from whence
this great river is derived, occupys the greatest part of this
side of the country, and at first was the finest hunting

country in all America; but the contests between the English and French Indians have so depeopled the stocks, that it hardly affords either beaver, or martins, or porcupines, or other family creatures. As to fish and fowl, and deer and foxes, wolves, bears, and woolvereens and catts, they are errattick, and constantly move with the seasons; but the family creatures are stationary, and 'tis the stocks of these whom those dissentions have distroyd.

On the shores of this great river, and on the lakes adjacent, the Outáwais occupie, and are a distinct tribe; a warlike people, and a terrour to all the neighboureing Indians; either tributary or in alliance with the Irroquois; and do neither trade with the Company nor the French; but go annually with the Irroquoos to trade with them at the Brittish setlements on the Lake Ontario. You will perhaps be a litle surprised that no other have taken notice of this; how extreemly kind I have been to this warlike Notoways, or Otáwais, in assigning them so large a trackt of country; but these powerfull people are such a terrour to the servile tribes, that although they do not constantly go annually a Usquemow hunting for their bloody inhumane sacrifice, those poor creatures do this for them, or are sure to be that sacrifice for themselves; and these, when procured, are to be tendred to the heads of the five nations of Irroquois, or Eliquoes, to be distributed to these very Notawais, or Otáwais. An instance of this I have before me: these very Indians sends word to Esquowenow, our captain, at Moose River, by two French Indians, that they wanted some Usquemows for their annuall sacrifice, and that he and his young men must provide them against such a moon, or be that sacrifice themselves.

Accordingly, he poor Esquowenow declares the war-dance in the year 1748, and away they go with great alacrity, and succeeded, and brought seven alive and thirteen scalps in great tryumph, and accordingly distributes his prizes, and order'd those two French Indians to carry a portion of them to the Irroquoos (or Eliquoes, as our Indians call them), and which those very Otawais refuse to take, but from the hands of the five nations; none of poor Esquoenows young men cared to undertake this dangerous embassie; which when he was informed that his sacrifice was favourably accepted, he (Esquoenow) publishes his feast, and there regales themselves over these horrid inhumane commons quite debonnair. This matter of fact I relate from those that were eye witnessis of it, and do sufficiently evince what I before advancid, and shew us of what consequence it would be to our trade if we could win these people over to the Companys intrest, what a fine frontier they would make us against the incursions of the wood runners.

Near the mouth of this great river is one other river, which takes a more easterly course, and is said to afford more water, with fewer sharps and falls, and by much more frequented by the servile tribes of natives, and is by the English Ruperts River, where was made the first setlement for the Company, called Charles's Fort; some time after, by the advise of the natives, our people found it necessary to go over to the west main to setle, and took Moose River by the way, and made a setlement there, but were dispossesed of it by the French, and demollished it in the beginning of King Williams reign, and lay so unoccupied untill the year 1732 the Company resumed a setlement, as is before mentioned. But the setlement at Albany has been thought so convenient and so commodious for trade, so secure a situation from the attempts of an enemy, that the trade here has been always so considerable as engage the Companys whole attention, throughout that long warr after the French had wrested every other part of the bay from them, at a prodigious expence and loss, which was confirmed to them afterwards by the treaty of Utrecht, and all Hudsons Bay beside. Near the mouth of these two rivers, to westward of Mount Shad-

8

dock, is a cluster of islands, caled Reids Islands; the westermost is caled little wood Isle, which lyes north from Point
Comfort, nine mile between which and the Point is the best
chanile into these two rivers; not but there is a good chanile
along the eastern shore near Mount Shaddock (which is the
highest land on this coast, and seen indifferently from Point
Comfort, from Charleton Sound, and from Strattons, and
near Slude River), and so down fourteen miles south to a
small, bold, bluff island, called Redunda, from hence by
edging to eastward, you fall into Ruperts River, and holding
down more southerly, you come into Notoway or Otáwais
River, but these have been disused many years, ever since
Grimingtons time, from whence I have these notes; to wester-
ward of this rivers mouth is a creek, caled Onengham, a
winter harbour, places the first voyagers made use: the
mouth of these rivers is in latitude 51° 20′ N., and seventy-
five miles to eastward of the north point of Moose River.

From Indian Head due north to the south end of Charleton
in latitude 51° 57′, on the east side of which is a charming
sound, fourteen miles in length, and winds round to eastward
of an unequall breadth, and cover'd by two woody islands,
caled Danby's and Caries, after king Charles's courtiers,
where Captain James wintered in that tattered condition he
himself discribes in Harriss's *Colection of Voyages*, to which
I refer.   Uppon this fine island the Company had a ware-
house many years in the time of the war, and sent but one
ship annually from England, where the factors from the east
main, Ruperts, Moose, and Albany rivers, came here with
their trade in sloops to meet the ship from England, and
there receive their supplys for each setlement, under the
conduct and assortment of one cheiff, who made out the
generall dispatches from whence the ship proceeded to England, but this was also disused after the French had dis-
posesed them of all but Albany, long before the end of the
warr, and that setlement was taken and retaken, and once

repulsed, but a few years before the end of Queen Anns reign.

Fourteen miles west from the south end of Charlton is the Rock of Lisbon, between whom are many shoalds and banks, so that in sailing from the westward you must take care to travel well to southward before you enter the sound, to avoid the dredfull ———.[1]

Eight miles from the north end are two small sandy islands, caled Gull Islands.

Futher ly's, or according to Grimington, Trodely's,[2] a fine, high, bold island, four mile in length, twenty-five miles E.S.E. from the Gaskitt, and N. by E. thirty-two miles from the Rock of Lisbon.

Twenty-three miles east from Trodely's are two small islands, called Struttons, which forms a fine sound or harbour, caled Phips's; between these and Trodeleys, about half way, are two small sandy islands without other names; the reefs and shoalds from these low sandy islands have always prevented our people from striking across through those islands, and are sure to stopp at Struttons and Charletons sounds in the passage to and from Slude River to Albany.

Trodely, in latitude 52° 40′, is uppon the same meridian of Solimons Temple, another island, four mile long, of a moderate height, and lyes E. by N. twenty-three miles from the Gaskitt.

Lord Westons islands, four in number, is thirteen miles N.N.W. from Solimons Temple, in latitude 53° 00′, and are seven miles in length, uppon the westermost of which the Company lost a ship 1724.

The Twinns south end is N.W. from Westons Islands six-

---

[1] Sentence incomplete in the manuscript.

[2] So in the manuscript. There are many sentences in the manuscript carelessly constructed, and words evidently omitted, from which the editor infers that Captain Coats's remarks have been badly copied, and are not in his own handwriting.

teen miles distant, N.E. by E. eighteen miles from the Horn
of Agomisco; the two islands are about sixteen miles in
length, with a small sound between, and a litle rock which
makes a good road; from the south end of the North Twinn
is a reef of rocks runs S. by E. five miles, where one of our
ships was hooked in in the year 1732, and indeed more than
ordinary care is to be used in sailing through these narrows,
where the tides throw you off to eastward on both sides of
Agomisco into deep water, and shouldens so suddenly, that
you cannot depend on going clear one mile, and therefore
you are to be free with Agomisco, and never go into deaper
water than is before observed; all along the northern side is
a flatt even sounding a good way off, untill you come to the
eastern point, or Horn, where you fall into broken ground
and deap water, ten to thirty fathom; in two or three casts
of the lead, from this point, in 53° latitude to 53° 30′, on a
W.N.W. course, you sail from twenty-two to eight fathom
very safely.

This islands form is like a weavers shutle, whose lateral
side faces the north, and the curvalinear covers the south,
where herds of dear are all the summer, where our home
Indians go to kill and dry quantitys of it for their and ours
uses at Albany; the interior parts is covered with wood, but
towards the skirts and borders is an unbounded fens and
marshes, which is cover'd with fowl; near the western extremity it is not above ten or twelve mile from the west main,
but is so choaked with banks and shoals, as make it unna-
vigable, yet 'tis said here is a brisk tide setts through; I
leave this to my readers reflection. Uppon the west main, in
53° 10′, is a river, caled by the natives Kickovan, pretty
considerable breadth and depth, but runs but a little way
into the country; is quite out of use. Farther northward is
a bay, caled Equan Bay, with pritty deep water, remarkable
for dcluding you into it in foggy weather, if you creep too
near the western coast in your progress along shore from the

northward, and therefore, as I before said, you must never neglect your lead day nor night.

Peters River, six miles east from Rock Redunda, is a small river, remarkable for nothing but the name of a pragmatical taylor : the coast lyes from hence to Mount Shaddock, nearly north and south, and covered with rocks and small islands innummerable.

Twenty mile east from Charleton, is a fine bold island caled Savage, to eastward of which is a cluster of many islands, where our first worthys first saw the natives.

The coast from Mount Shaddock falls of to eastward about N.N.E., and covered by many islands alway to Slude River, in latitude 52° 10′ N., where the company has a factory on the south entrance, and winters a sloop every year, to which those servil tribes come from all parts of Labrodore to trade here, except those in the French interest. This river expatiates, by its branches, into the lakes of Saquina, who give us allarms frequently ; but as they, the French, have got most of the trade of this country, down to the Otawais, they are too politick to give us farther provocation, or what we have may appear to them too considerable. Ours, principly, is from the northern Indians, who border on the Usquemows, and is, one year with another, near three thousand skins, mostly small furrs, which, by a day in June, are embarqued in the sloop, and sent to Albany, to be repacked in their cargo, and so sent home.

These northern Indians border uppon the Usquemows, and live in a sort of servile frindship with them ; but are nothing like those northern Indians I mentioned at Churchill. These are neither so brave in their persons, nor so prudent in their manners, but are an easy, indocill, broken, abject people, who have been cruelly ravaged by the Usquemows, with whom at present at peace : but the inroads of the more southern tribes in their rambles, a Usquemow hunting for their bloody inhumane sacrifices, have broke and depeopled,

altho' frinds, more than there natural enimies the Usquemows, when these poor people often make good their disap-
pointment, and so are butchered for God's sake.

All the bays, and rivers, and lakes, and creeks, abound
with salmon, trout, titimegg, jack, and perch, etc., and dear,
and fowl, and partridges, more plenty full then any where
else: foxes, martins, otters, are by much the finest in Hudsons
Bay. As these correspond with the Usquemow, we find they
like iron, and iron tools, and fishing tackle, beyond any other
thing; but by the intercourse of the French, they have
picked up there guegaws, and gimcracks, and begin to be as
fond as the others.

Cape Hope, in latitude 52° 40′, are one larger, and several
small islands, N.W. by W., twenty-seven miles from George's
Point, fifty miles east from the Gaskitt, in which is a fine
cove, secure from all winds, but the south-east, where, formerly, the annuall ship wintered : it affords some fish, and
plenty of wood, but inconvenient for many other necessary's.

Those people had such dreadfull apprehensions of the
deluges in all the rivers, that they always grapled with great
difficultys; so far from the main, where must be had every
refreshment, but now is made tolerable, if not desireable, by
taking another method.

Gibbs's Island is in latitude 52° 55′ N., fifteen miles due
from Cape Hope, and two larger, and divers lesser ; to east-
wards of whom, near the main, ly's anothers cluster of islands,
called Gilpins, eight miles east from Gibbs's, where Captain
James Knight[1] wintered in the year 1692, with one hundred

---

[1] Captain James Knight (the governor of the Factory at Nelson's
River) conducted an expedition for the discovery of a rich copper mine,
in the years 1719-21. They all met with a melancholy end ; and half
century passed away before their remains were found on Marble Island,
Chesterfield Inlet. It is stated that in the second winter their numbers
were reduced from fifty to twenty, and that in the following summer
only five remained, three of whom did not long survive. The two who
remained, frequently ascended a rock to look for relief, and would sit

and twenty-three men, a monument of which stands erected to this day.

Sheppards Island is, south from Gibbs's, about five or six miles, and fifty-two miles E. by S. from Westons Islands, and seventy-five miles E. by S. from the Horn of Agomisco. They are tolerably high, with some wood upon them.

Grimmingtons Bay, where he winterd severall times, in latitude 53° 10′, is fifteen miles from the north to south, with many nameless islands in it. The coast lyes nearly north and south, and is covered with innumerable litle islands, rocks, and shelves, to a considerable distance from the shore.

Trout River, in 53° 40′, runs a good way into the country, whence is taken abundance that fish, which was a great refreshment to Grimington and his men.

Sea-Horse Point, near the entrance of this river, is a long point of stones, remarkable for being cover'd with those creatures at perticular seasons.

Mishshegattee, or the Great River, is in 54° 10′ N., and extends into the inland lakes, as its name imports. This river, we are told, by its branches and lakes, affords an easy communication with the Eastern Ocean ; and Saquina River abounds with sturgeon, white whales, and all the other species of fish.

The northern Indians before mentioned, would gladly draw us to setle on this river, to get farther from the French Indians ; and that the Usquemows would come there to trade, which would make us amends for loosing those few Indians we have from the skirts of Ruperts River, and the parts adjacent. 'Tis said here is to be had izing glass, christial, and lead ore, which, when one considers what a

down on their return and weep bitterly. At last (so we are told), one of the two sunk under his misfortunes, and the other died while digging his grave. How all these particulars are handed down to us is not quite clear ; and the latter part of the story is, no doubt, a fabrication ; but that the whole of the poor fellows died off, there is no reason to doubt.

track't of land this noble capacious river runs through, is less to be wondered att.[1]

From hence the coast winds out to westward, nearly N.N.W., to Cape Jones, in latitude 55° 00', and is the eastern promontary, as Cape Henritta Maria is the western of James Bay, and is one hundred and fifty miles to eastward of that west main. Very many shoalds, and islands, and embarrissments, covers this coast, that we cannot explain it so fully as we could wish ; and many islands have been new named, and those so named still more doubtfull, that we shall sum up all we have to say,—that near the cape is a high broken land, and the coast to northward declines to eastward, nearly N.E., as it does to southward nearly S.S.E. Near all those islands there is tolerable anchorage, and good shelter under some of them. Here is very litle tide, and seldom flows above two foot, but runs to northward always, if not disturbed by the winds.

Our two sloops, in there progress to Artiwinepeck in 1744, hauled in with this cape, and found a fine chanile between those ranges of islands and the main for upwards of twenty leagues, nearly north-east, and rode and named sundry islands in their progress to Great White Whale River, in 55° 23' N. latitude, with a fine entrance, and a most capacious river, abounding with all sorts of fish, of flesh, and fowl; where those northern Indians reside all the summer, as well as the greatest part of the winter. This river, by the concurrent testimony of all the Indians, is said, by its lakes and branches, to fall into the Eastern Ocean.[2] Upon the shores of this river is to be had the finest island christial I ever saw, grows solitary, in multangular forms, of an

---

[1] *Note by Captain Coats.*—Sequescom says, it runs E. by S. one hundred miles into a large lake one hundred and twenty miles over from east to west ; and that on the eastern verge Saquinay issues down to Canada, and is full of sharps and falls; that on the northern and southern borders are branches into other lakes.

[2] This is not correct, as it falls into James's Bay.

exceeding fine water ; lead oar, and izinglass in many places.

These provident Indians reside on this river, where they catch and cure quantities of fish ; try up the oyl,[1] and is said to be very palateable, at least not distaistefull when done there way. No Indians in America have a greater affluence and plenty than these, and without rambling those immense countrys the others do ; and would be very numerous, was it not for those diobolical principles that delude those honest, good-natured, idle, indolent, happy people, which shatters and breaks the spirits of these, which are so obnoxious to frinds and foes. The Company has been made sensible of this, but could not fall on a way sooner to shelter these unhappy people ; which, in all probability, our new setlement at Artiwinipeck will be a means to protect them, and ennable them to keep in a body, by carrying all they want to their doors. In the latitude 55° 50', is a noble, high, bold island, named the Bill of Portland, N.W. by N., eleven mile from the north check of that river; farther to northward is another island, caled Merry's, in honour of one of the gentlemen of the committee ; afford good anchorage between them and the main. From hence is nothing remarkable untill you come to Litle Whale River, on the N.E. crs. in latitude 56° 08', with high bold land on each side a going in. Over a bar, with eight foot uppon it in the midle, is a sunken rock, dry at half-tide, which flows here about four foot water. About two mile within the barr, this river divides into two branches ; one lesser takes a more easterly cours, the larger one a more southerly crs.; but are both terminated by falls impassable to any thing but canoes, one mile above the Fork Point. Adjacent to the lesser creek, four miles up, on the side of a very high cliff, is that fine lead-mine so much taken notice off ; but is so difficult to bring down, that when above twenty men was employed to get it down, they

---

[1] So in the manuscript.

had not above three tons and half, although near three
weeks about it.   There is the finest christials in the world
there ; there is vast shoals of white whale there, and other
fish in great plenty ; pritty woddy within, and much grass.
N. by E. from this rivers mouth, is a bold island, five leagues
dist. named Bibyos ; from whence, S.S.W. three mile, runs
a ledge of rock.   The coast is rocky quite to Gulph Hazard,
in latitude 56° 22′ N., distant about sixteen mile N.E. by
N., where is such a race that the Indians have found a
most expressive word for, Qua-qua-chick-iwan,—it swallows
quickly.   Belchers Islands, four in number, lyes forty-five
leagues to westward of Litle Whale River ; by another
account, only twenty-nine leagues, in latitude 56° 06′, where
I was entangled three days in ice.   I found a flood and ebb
setting due east and west ; but we drove to eastward most.
I have made a computation of about four and a half miles a
day.   This increment to eastward, which is owing to those
vast quantities of snow, which disolves and drains down our
rivers from the western shore, amongst whom is good anchor
ground.

   About seven leagues north from those is a range of islands
twenty leagues in length, fourteen larger, and many smaller ;
the midle, in 58° 00′ N. latitude, at the distance of seventeen leagues from the east main, amongst which the Usquemows swarms all the summer months to catch fish and
moulted fowl, in great abundance, uppon all these, Belchers
and Sleeper islands.   In latitude 59° 05′, we told fourteen
islands in sight ; and, by my account, the westermost is
uppon the same meridian of the North Bear ; and the North
Bear is 2° 50′ west longitude from Cape Diggs ; and Gulph
Hazard lyes 2° 05′ east longitude from Cape Diggs, in 56° 22
north latitude.

   The Sleepers are seven larger, and many smaller islands,
from 59° 40′ to 60° 05′ ; the westermost is in 59° 50′, and is
fourteen miles to westward of the North Bear, with fine

opnings and good anchorage; and many Usquemows haunt
these islands in summer, and bears S.W. by S. twenty-three
leagues from Cape Smith; a high, bold, noble cape may be
seen twenty-five leagues.

In latitude 61° 40′ N., is the south-west point of Mansfield,
fourteen miles to eastward of the West Sleeper, and bear
from the south-east point W. by S. eighteen miles; is extreamly low and flatt, and has neither bush nor brake; but
all round these parts you have good soundings on both sides,
to 61° 00′ of latitude southerly, where you cross a ridge of
hard ground, some ten leagues from east to west, from
twenty-five to forty-five fath. into soft ground to eastward,—
a very usefull observation in coming from the westward.
The south-east part is ninety-six miles S.W.½W. from Cape
Digg.

From the south end of Mansfield, on both sides, is low
even ground, and pritty good soundings; but as you go
more northerly, the land is higher, and the coast is deaper
and rocky, and forty fatham is near enough on the east side,
and twenty-five fatham on the west side. Near the midle,
on the east side, are two small islands, which would afford a
good harbour. The N.W. part is fifteen leagues from Diggs.

On the north end, in latitude 62° 35′, is an inlet of a good
breadth, and runs in some distance; but I think the other is
preferable. The coast all round the north end of Mansfield
is deap water and foul ground, and rocky. On the north-
west part of this island is a patch of snow, about one mile
square, which, in hazy weather, is to be seen when you cannot see the island. I named it Silver Patch.

There is such swarms of fowl here, uppon this island, that
it seems incapable to contain them; which we meet at sea
many leagues off, before we see the island. The Usquemow
do vizet this island also, and for the same reason. This
island, in its form, is not unlike a nine-pin, with its apex to
the north, and winds both ways to its base, nearly S.W. by S.

twenty leagues : in latitude, the S.W. point lyes on the same
meridian of the North Bear; the westermost of Bakers
Dozen, in latitude 58° 20′ N., lyes four mile to westward of
this point; and the West Sleeper, in 59° 50′, is fourteen mile
to westward of this point, and lyes eighty-six miles to westward of Cape Diggs.

Cape Pembroke, as has been said, is a high cliff, in latitude
63° 05′ N.; lyes fifty-seven miles to westward of the midle
of the north end of Mansfield, seventy-six miles more to
Cape Walsingham, and eighteen miles to the east end of
Salisbury, and one hundred and forty-nine east from thence
to the west end of Cape Charles : one about four leagues
distant, and the other five leagues; so that this note says
these two lands are one hundred and seventy-six miles, east
and west, from each other.

From Cape Pembroke to Carieswansnest, in latitude 62° 10′,
and longitude 7° 13′ west from Cape Diggs, or two hundred
miles, is an even champain, barren country, without bush or
brake, or anything remarkable, save an island named Cape
Nesdrake, where the coast wind about more to westward on
the south side, as it does more to northward on the north
side. In the year 1737 I made many observations on this
coast, which corooberated so well with Foxs, which I litt of
afterwards, that I was greatly pleased; and found a languid
flood and ebb, which I lost entirely after I passed Caries-
swansnest. At Cape Nesdrake it run one and eight-tenths
of a mile; and at Carieswansnest, seven-tenths of a mile.
This is matter of fact, from many essays. From Carieswansnest to Cape Nesdrake, the coast is east and west, nearly a
broken rocky shore, and forty fatham is near enough; you
have sixty fatham four leagues off the coast. From thence
to Cape Pembroke, the coast is somewhat higher; Carieswansnest is a most dangerous cape land. I had one hundred
and twenty fatham not above five leagues from it. It is very
low land, and the coast declines both ways many points; so

that you must depend entirely on your latitude, which I have
sett down with some degrees of accuracy. Cape Southampton is said to ly more northerly and to westward, to which I
can say but litle : only when we speak of it, we call it the
Southampton Shore, the Southampton Coast, etc.

This Carieswansnest lyes one hundred and fourteen miles
to westward of the south-west part of Mansfield Island, but
makes a narrower chanile nearest the north end, as the coast
inclines to each other. This chanile I have named the Boke
of Mansfield, which has deap water on both sides, and a very
low, dangerous coast : add to this, your southerly winds are
generally foggy, and those shores collect those opaque
vapours, which are drove through here from all the southern
and western parts of the bay ; so likewise 'tis more liable to
blowing tempestious weather. And as you must encounter
with these difficultys, you will expect I should give what aid
and light I can. In coming into this chanile from the southward, you may be out in your latitude as well as your longitude ; and therefore it will be necessary to take your soundings uppon the south end of Mansfield, to southward of
latitude of 62° 00′ N., for after you are to northward, you
fall into deap water eighty or one hundred fatham, unless
you come near either shore ; if to southward of that latitude,
you have not less than one hundred and twenty fatham.
Uppon the Southampton Coast, if to northward of that latitude, you shoalden quickly ; if to eastward, on the island
side, you fall into a deaper water, with a N.E. course, which
declines from the island ; and if on the Southampton side
you shoalden, which you may satisfie your self by traversing
two or three miles so entred, you boldly sail into 63° 00′ latitude, and then you haill to eastward S.E., or S.E. by E., for
the entrance of Hudsons Streights.

When you come from the westward, the difficulty is the
same ; you must not dare go to northward of 62° 00′ N.,
least you fall on the west side of that low cape land, nor much

to southward, least you lose the benefitt of those soundings on that shore, which are so convenient for entring this channile. If you think it convenient to run to eastward of Mansfeild, you may most comodiously run to eastward in 61° 00′, or 61° 20′ N., and may depend on meeting that ridge I before mentioned from the south of Mansfeild; and then hale N.N.E., or N.E. by N., will bring you to Cape Diggs. This was the method they followed formerly; but we lately have been at liberty to go indifferently on either side of Mansfeild; and the channiles are both nearly of a breadth, but the northerly winds in the fall, makes it necessary to use the western, not the eastern chanile. In stormy wether, y'll tell me it is very troublesome to keep your lead in such deap water : it is so, but after yo come into forty or fifty fatham, you verge on either side; and, therefore, this precaution is not to be neglected in dark nor gloomy wether, otherwise, if it is clear, you sail as near either shore as you please, for I dont know of any banks or shoalds at any great distance from the shore.

Shark Point, N. by E. from Cape Pembroke, in latitude 63° 30′, and in longitude 84° 30′ west from London, and so on to Cape Comfort, in latitude 65° 00′ N., and longitude 86° 10′ west from London, are remarkable, for giving the antient worthys some pleasure[1] when they found the coast wind round to westward, but falling into a bay more northerly : Fox calls it his farthest. These three cape lands, and this bay, makes west side of the North Channile ; as Lord Westons Portland, in 66° 30′ north latitude, and longitude 81° 30′ west from London ; twenty leagues south-east from which is Cape Dorchester ; twelve leagues south-east farther

---

[1] Whatever pleasure the ancient worthies may have derived upon this coast, certain it is, that it has not been vouchsafed to those of modern times. It was off this coast, from Cape Comfort to Seahorse Point, that Sir George Back was beset in the Pack, in the "fearful voyage of the *Terror*," in 1837, when he miraculously escaped shipwreck.

is Cape Charles, makes the eastern side of that North Channile.

Robert Bilot afterwards attempted this place, and got up
into 66° 47′ N. on the western side of this channile ; but in
traversing here, he found but thirty-five fatham ; and finding
the land wind away to eastward, and much incumbred with
ice, and allso a broken tide, from Cumberlands Inlet, as he
supposes, he quitted the western land to avoid the indraught
of that inlet, and stood into Caukins Sound, in 65° 40′, where
it flow'd eighteen foot water ; and an E. by S. moon makes
full sea.   To northward of these places, no Europeons, if
ever, penetrated from Hudsons Bay or Streights (except
Midleton in Sir Thomas Roes Wellcome).   But if we compare this with Wm. Baffin in his bay, he traversed from Sir
James Lancaster's Sound along that western coast, from
70° 30′ N. latitude, to 68° 00′ N., and saw that western land,
but was obliged to forsake it for the same reason, impassable
ice : thus these three worthys saw, but could not accomplish that most desireable discovery—not into the south
sea's, but joyn Hudsons to Baffins Bay ; and all agree to
northward of Lord Westons Portland the land winds away
to eastward.   If Fox's longitude be true, and you compare
it with Middletons in Repulse Bay, you will find that these
three persons were pritty near each other, altho different in
their rout ; for in that bay to northward of Cape Comfort,
they had but litle tide, and not very shallow water, and that
ice, not land, prevented their going further to westward ; also,
it flow'd but litle water.   Fox says, a S. by E. moon makes full
sea at Shark Point ; and Midleton says, a west moon, at his
frozen streights, makes full sea.   The bay was full of ice
when Fox and Bilot was there ; and the frozen streights has
not been clear since the creation, accordingly to Middleton,
of ice.   The others lost the sett of a tide as soon as they past
Cape Comfort ; and Middleton cales his Repulse Bay a Mill
Pond, in one expression, so that they corroberate in every

circumstance, only in his unnatureall deduction of the times of high water, which it is impossible to reconcile with an eastern tide. I put no retraint uppon nature, but take the matter of fact as they stand recorded in their own accounts: examine them yourselves; it appears so to me. I am not more surprised at Middletons asserting this matter of facts, then at Mr. Dobbs for not putting that controversie to issue about his frozen streights and the northestern tide he so much laboured, uppon the identity of those circumstances.

These are such glaring oversights in two such able persons, as shall be an instance to futurity how mens judgement may be injured by heat, by resentment, and by a too partial influence to this, or that side of the question.

Salisbury Islands, Notingham Islands, and Mill Island, remains to be spoke too. Salisbury Island is in latitude 63° 25′ N., thirty-seven miles to eastward of Cape Diggs, and fifty-eight miles to westward of the east end of Cape Charles, and one hundred and eighty miles to eastward of Cape Pembroke; 'tis a high bold island, about twelve miles long, south, from the east end; six miles distance, is a litle rock as bigg as a ship, with very deap water round it. Betwen this and Notingham runs a brisk tide thro a sound six miles over: the southermost part is in latitude 63° 15′ N.; is north from Cape Diggs thirty-six miles; is coverd with many litle islands, which distract the tide in various directions. Sir Thomas Button was at anchor in this sound, and was so farr deluded by the direction of this tide, that he made such deductions there from, as do but litle credit to his memory. This island is eight leagues in length from the north-west to south-east; from the east of Salisbury to the east of Notingham the course is W.S.W. eight or nine leagues, and the west end is in latitude 63° 50′ N., and bears from that cape N.N.W.

N.N.W. from Cape Diggs, in latitude 64° 28′, are four islands, caled by Fox, Mill Islands, from the ice grinding uppon them. Cape Charles, on the eastern side of the North Channile, is twelve leagues N.E. from these islands ; these islands, and the main to eastward of the North Channile, are all high, bold, montanious land, and are indinted in bays and coves, and the hills are cut and interspersed with valeys, very foul, and rocky, and deap water, every where near them.

Many tribes of Usquemows haunt and reside in these islands, whose shores are cover'd with fowl; and seas abound with some black whale, many sea-horses, seals, and all sorts of oyl fish, salmon, and some others.

The Usquemows[1], all over the streights, are bold, robust, hardy people, undaunted, masculine men, no tokens of poverty or want, with great fat, flatt, greazy faces, litle black percing eyes, good teeth, lank, black, matted hair, with litle hands and feet, under proportion; a well made back and shoulders; loyns, buttock, and haunces, well fortified; thighs are pretty full, but their leggs taper into a litle foot.  *  *

\*       \*       \*       \*       \*

There women weare such an uncouth habitt, as make it extreamly difficult for them to move about at all; their shoes, boats [boots], and breaches, are all of a peice, sett of to an extravigant breadth at top, which holds a child, and half their houshold furniture in each ; her mantua is divers skins, sow'd like our seamens frocks, a head like a monks cawl, but large enough to put a child in, as well as her head ; this comes

---

[1] The correctness of Captain Coats, in his description of the features of these Esquimaux, is entirely corroborated by Captain Lyon, in his narrative of his unsuccessful attempt to reach Repulse Bay in the *Griper*, in the year 1824. It is impossible to look at the clever sketches which Captain Lyon has introduced in his book, without seeing how faithful is the description Captain Coats has given of their " great, fat, flatt, greazy faces, little black percing eyes, good teeth," etc.; and in speaking of them, Captain Lyon calls them, " boisterous, noisy, fat fellows."—*Brief Narrative of an unsuccessful attempt to reach Repulse Bay through Sir Thomas Rowe's Welcome, in H.M. ship Griper, in the year* 1824. By Captain G. F. Lyon, R.N., p. 128.

10

down to her breach, and is decorated with party coloured
skins, and sowed very neat all along the borders, at breast
and hands, with a long tail, three foot and a half long, about
six inches broad in the crutch, and, as it farther depends, may
be ten inches broad, decorated likewise with a litle loop at
the end, which is rounded off: its use is too apparent in so
rigorous a clime to need any further explanation; under this,
they weare a litle pair of breeches, close behind, and before
goes half way down their thighs, and under all, weare a
smok, made of bladder and beast gut, curiously dry'd, and
sow'd very neat, or dear skin, made thin, and not badley
dressed, with two or three pair of socks, and their hair ty'd
in a roll uppon the fore heads. In this garb, this happy
people enjoy a contentment not to be purchased by rubies.
The habits of the men are not much different; their shoes
and boats tyd under the knee; their breaches a litle longer;
their coats not so long, nor so long a tail to them; their cawl
for their head less, and made to pull over their broad faces
pritty tite, as the skirts are made to draw over a hoop (the
only aperture into their close canoes), in the midle where he
sitts, not much unlike a weavers shutle, if both sides were
made curvilinear; he has one padle, nine or ten foot long,
with blades at each end, fortified on the edges with bone or
ivory; thus accutred, they will dart past the ships at a prodigious rate, at least fourteen or sixteen mile an hour, re-
gardles of wind or sea, for nothing can enter his canoe while
he keeps his seat. They have many contrivances to catch
fowl and kill fish of the most ennormous size, very ingenious
and curious, and with great facility. These canoes are so
tender, and composed of so many litle peices of wood, of
whale bones, and bones of fish and beasts, as would asstonish
you how they held together; and, lastly, they draw over this
peice bitt frame, a covering of skins, made tite all over, and
sow'd on close every where to that hoop where its lord sits in
pride and hauty contempt. I have often thought this people are

of the linage of the Chinese, in the many features I think I see in them—their bloated, flatt faces, litle eyes, black hair, litle hands and feet, their listlessness to travilling, very fair when free from greese, very submissive to their men, very tender of their children, and are indefatigable in the gew gaws to please their men and children. I have had some of those toys from the children brought to me by father and mother, to learn them to look at us without trembling, which shew this peoples great wisdom. These toys are litle peices of ivory, made in form of all their fishes, all their fowls, all their beasts, all their utensils, men, women, and children; nay, some to imitate our ships, our boats, and our men, litle canoes, luggage boats, litle bows and arrows; in short, nothing escapes their notice; and even in these childess things, bestow a good deal of labour. As they get vast numbers of seals, sea-horses, and deer skins, so most of their habitts are made of one or other of those skins.

The want of wood, and severity of the clime, puts this people on eating their victuals raw; not but we have had litle stone pots and bone spoons, and other contrivances to dress victuals; but this, I suppose, may be for their sick or children only, for 'tis not possible to gett fewell for that use. Blubber and seals flesh make up the greatest part of their food; not but that they easily catch fowl of all sorts, and other fish what they please, and do live in great affluence and plenty, and would not, I am persuaded, change their fatt dabbs for all the fine luxurys of the east.

It has been said that these are Anthropophagions, and that their cruelty and barbarity is not to be expressed. I answer, it is no otherwise than as all the Indians in America do, to sacrifice their enimyes to their god; and then, indeed, they do partake of human flesh. But to say it is a delicate, and that they do it at any time when they can gett it, and that it is a favorite dish, I believe 'tis quite otherwise; for my own part, I see nothing in them to countenance such a hellish

principle, and do think them as gentle and sociable, and more
so, since one cave often serves a whole tribe of two or three
hundred persons, men, women, and children, where they
live in love and affection, and more unanimous than we can
pretend too; so obliging and so affectionate to one another,
when we are trading with them, that any person may perceive what a harmony there is amongst them.

That they are idoliters, I am perswaided; for I have had
a bone deity, which they seldom are without in their canoes.
The rising sun summons all on their knees, when you hear
such a contrast of vocal musick as comes from the lowest
recessis of the mind, with such energy and noble contempt
as lift these people, in idea, above the common leval of all
mankind; and I daresay they think themselves the favorite
people of God, and look on us with more compassion and
contempt than we do them. For to what reason can we
ascribe that great confidence in them, when they singly and
alone have put themselves in my hands, but a nobleness of
mind, above the low conceits of mean earthly creatures? All
our shining characters in history had this criterion,—suspi-
cion, and jealousy, and diffidence, are always esteemed the
true intimations of a pusillanimous. Nor does this great
confidence[1] and resignation proceed from stupidity, as I
observed at Ice Cove; for while we conversed with these
people, both men, women, and children, with all the freedom
and cheerfullness in the world, yet, as soon as our people
shewed them they wanted to look into their tents, and trans-
gress the laws of decorum, in one instant the women and
children retired, and the men had their bows and arrows in
their hands as quick as thought; which, when I perceived,

---

[1] Captain Lyon, in his voyage of the *Griper*, speaks thus of the great
confidence of these poor Esquimaux :—" As we walked to them along
high shingly beaches intersecting small swampy lakes, several birds were
shot by our officers ; but although the natives saw them fall, they expressed neither surprise, fear, nor curiosity, about the guns."—*Brief
Narrative*, p. 57.

I caled of our men at the intreaty of one old man, and so
the women and children came again to their gambols with
our people, as before, debonair, and in good humour, and
before we parted, brought us two or three dozen of young
green geese, and came on board the ships severall times
afterwards whilst we stayed there. These instances shew
these people are not stupid; but their confidence and resignation is in a higher power,—that power we are taught to
dread, but to dispise all others. So that in these people you
see practical philosophers; what we should be, what we are
not. How mean and contemptable must we appear in the
eyes of these people! who, when we approach them with
crouds, and caution, and bustle, and noise, and firing of
guns, enough to terrifie such hen-hearted creatures as we
are, which makes no other impression on them than extort
a laugh, and hasten their way towards us. I have often
thought that the book of nature is more evident to them than
us. The inferiour creatures betray their fear by squeaking,
chirping, running, or scratching; but lyons, bulls, bears,
egles, whales, sharks, and wolves, shew no signs of fear, but
go on uniform in all their habitts and motions unaffected with
fear, invariable in their gratification of sense. If, as the
philosophers say, that man, in his composition and passions,
partakes of all the beasts of the forest, how different are ours
to these savages, as we call them! In these is such a serenity
and composedness on every occasion (not but they are very
fond of iron),[1] that I have often beheld them with great
admiration. This is the character of our Usquemows in
Hudsons Streights and Bay, and am sensible 'tis somewhat

---

[1] This is probably a quaint insinuation of their pilfering propensities,
which are not to be denied. Captain Lyon says, that some of the natives
who visited his ship were not so violently overpowered by their joyous
sensations as to forget that they came to improve their fortunes; and one
most expert fellow succeeded pretty well in picking pockets, an occupa-
tion from which frequent detection did not discourage him.—*Lyon's
Brief Narrative*, etc., p. 37.

different from Mr. Egedes in Straight Davis; but this may
be easily accounted for where a nation is broke by war or
other calamity. How soon it produces a degeneracy in the
people, we need not go from home to verify this instance.

My sentiments on this people has had so good effect on
the present gentlemen in the direction of the Company, that
in the year 1749 an attempt was made to setle amongst them,
and fix a factory, in such a situation as might secure our
people, and accomidate these people to trade. Accordingly
I was sent to survey the coast from Cape Diggs down the
Labrodore, and collect as many circumstances, and make
such observations, as was necessary to accomplish this design.

But found that coast so wild and barren to northward of
Gulph Hazard, in latitude 56° 22′ N., and longitude 2° 05′ E.
from Cape Diggs, that there was no possibility to subsist
Europeons to northward of that gulph, where we entred and
erected Richmond Fort, which will give us an easie access
to these people, and accomidate those wandring tribes of
northern Indians: a people hitherto greatly distressed for
want of a setlement to succour and support them from the
many enemies these poor people have on both sides. Thus
you have our endeavours. God must crown the intention.
We have watered; but God must give the increase. As the
motive is truly generous, so God will bless it with his aid.
The small share I have had in the execution of this laudable
design are entirely from motives of honour and conscience.
If I live to see it succeed, it will give me infinite pleasure;
if not, Gods will be done. Nothing from me shall ever
intervene; let those that do, be answerable for it. But
enough: 'tis time to resume the geography.

From Cape Diggs, in 64° 40′ N., and in longitude 79° 00′
west from London, down the Labrodore coast on the east
main, after you are the isles of Diggs Deception: eight leagues
S. by W. from that cape, you have a barren, levill, plain
country, all along to Cape Smith, in latitude 60° 47′ N.; and

seventeen mile to westward of Cape Diggs, which is a high,
bold, brave land, from whence extend a range of mountains,
E. by N., to an indetermined distance, which tower over
that barren, wild, fenny country.  To northward of that
cape, are nothing remarkable, but four islands, twelve leagues
to northward, caled Four Usquemows.

The shores is very foul and stoney all along within twenty
fatham water ; but without that, you have a clean oazy
bottam.

We anchored and sent our boats ashore at sundry places
on this coast, and found a gradual discent of the flood as we
proceeded to southward.  At Cape Smith, and at the Sound,
we found the current sett to northward perpetually, and that
the rising of water abaited something of its force, but run to
northward always.  It rise and fell about four foot water.

The sound is near two mile wide, and affords a fine harbour ; but the barren islands are so scattred in it, that you
are never above a quarter of a mile from one or other.  'Tis
a good eight mile through, and very rocky, and lyes much
exposed to a south-west wind.

In 61° 20′ are five islands, from whence we had some
Usquemows, who seem to me to be meeker and modester,
and of a more Indian complection, neither so robust and
hardy, nor so undaunted and insolent, as in the streights ; but
with a meek, resigned confidence, put themselves into my
hands, without diffidence or precaution—a strong evidence
of their innocence.  I take the more perticular notice of this,
because none of our ships ever touched here before.

Cape Smith, as was said, is a brave, high, bold promontary,
and extends itself, W. by S., six leagues from the adjacent
coast on the north side, and nine leagues from the adjacent
coast on the south side.

Fenny Coast, which is a very low fenny coast, from the
foot of that range of mountains before taken notice of, all
along the coast to the Point of Portland, in latitude 59° 00′,

and appears, here and there, with litle tufts and hammocks, as you sail along ashore ; but this coast is so lined with islands, banks, and broken ground, that it is not easy to come at it. There is no standing into less than twenty fatham, no where ; but you meet banks, and riges, and broken ground.

Near the Point of Portland, which is a high, bold promontary, in latitude 59° 00', and near the meridian of Cape Diggs, before which are a cluster of barren, bare islands, I named Duble Dozens, the westermost of whom I caled in memory of my habitation, Limehouse and Ratcliff, with deap water very near them, and foul anchorage. There runs a constant current to northward through them ; the water of gall colour, owing, as I conceive, to a large mixture of fresh water.

These islands are all of them craggy, cliffy, and riseing ground ; very ragged, and many sunken rocks amongst them, where you must be very cautious in sailing through. From hence the coast winds south-east, and pritty high land, and deap water, and is lined with islands, without distinction, to Hopwell Hoad, in 58° 00', and do make a fine chanile between these and the main, which may be of infinite use in times to come. I have named them Holmes of Hopwell.

From thence to Gulph Hazard, in latitude 56° 22' N., the coast is a brave, high, bold land—in some places montanious, with a botamless shore, and covered with a chain of islands, of sundry sizes, and are distinguished with names, as by the map annexed.

These islands form a fine channile, and fine anchorage, which I named Richmond Channiles. The islands covering these whole coast, to Cape Smith, affords a most comodious navigation for sloops, boats, and canoes ; and I doubt not but ships may find shelter in many places thro those numbles inlets, which is hardly less than from one mile to five mile wide, and an oazy bottam. The current all along this coast setts along shore to northward about two mile an hour, and

rises three foot water alternately. The variation of the nea-
dle in 1749, at Cape Diggs, 42° north-westerly, and at Gulph
Hazard, 29° north-westerly; at the south end of Mansfeild,
36° north-westerly, and at the intermediate distances, proportionable.

The whole coast, from Cape Diggs to Gulph Hazard, is so
wild and barren near the sea, that we hardly saw one living
thing, except a fuee crows, gulls, fish, fowl, sea pigeons, etc.
The land afforded a sort of rye grass, snow drops, white
and purple, without odur, and a creeping bramble, without
berrys. Southward of the point of Portland, the valleys grew
more salutary, and the grass and shrubs more mature; and
we found some berrys here and there, and amongst the stones,
many sparkling gems, which gave a luster to this barren,
silent, inhospitable country.

I remark that the grass seams of a better colour, of a more
lively green, not so pauled and burnt to southward, then it
is to northward of Cape Smith; that the shrubs are in a
small degree larger, and the grass is deeper in the valeys on
the south side. The barren, bare rocks which border this
whole coast, produces no living creature; even the snow
ponds which face the sun, and are sufficiently heated, has
not one living thing in them; no aquatick, no worm, no in-
sect, but muskeeta's; no berrys, no seed, no food for Gods
creatures, neither by land nor water, for we tryed our netts
every where. No wonder, so unreplenished by nature, it
should remain desolate.[1] And yet I am of oppinion, that the
fish of the sea, as well as beasts and fowls, are stationary no
where, but in their errattick rambles, may vizit this barren

[1] This desolate coast seems to bear a marked resemblance to that
discovered by Lieutenant Sherrard Osborn, late commanding H.M. Steam
Tender *Pioneer*, who conducted an extended party from Captain Austin's
squadron (1851), and penetrated south-west of Cape Walker, to latitude
71° 50', and longitude 104°, a distance of five hundred and six miles, from
the winter quarters of the squadron and back to the ships,—one of the
most remarkable journeys performed in the arctic regions.

soil. Their is some snow moss in the valeys, which, I am told, the dear are fond of; and nature produces nothing in vain. But I am perswaded their stay is but very short on so scanty commons what I have taken notice of. Doubtless, the natives Usquemows know the time and seasons of those haunts, and nick it, for we found vestiges of them at all the places we stopt att. And O, my consciouns! I think they are all gone together, for when we go ashore, there is so profound silence, such awefull precipices, no cackling, chirping, squeeking, on land or water; all nature seams asleep, that we could hardly immagine ourselves awake, and uppon the earth, untill we scale those lofty summits, and see those sparkling saphires, which display'd their glories on the face of the sun. The sea and sounds affords a fine prospect from thence.

I must add, in kindness, there is fine shelter for a ship in stormy weather, when it comes to be well known, in fine coves, fine sounds, and good anchorage; and that it may be vastly usefull hereafter, I have named those high hills of Hopwell, the islands, holins, and chanile, as is before taken notice of, the channile from twenty-five to five fatham, from two to four miles wide, this note says, and rounds and runs to the point of Portland upwards of twenty leagues; and I fore see it will be of great service to futurity in carrying on the Usquemow trade, which will shelter our traders from ice and storms in their passages early in the spring, when and before those wanderers retire from the main to their summer residence.

Gulph Hazard is not above two miles in length into Artiwinipeck, yet wind is of little service, the land is so tremendous high, and hang over the sound, that the wind, as well as the waters, are reverberated by those cliffs; mainly in this consists the danger, and where the sound is botamless, there are other difficulties, but I'll forbear to say more, because it opens into a fine expanse. The Artiwinipeck appears so finely variegated with mountains, groves, cascades, and cateracts,—vales so adorned, with trees and fine meddows interspersed here and there, that I was struck with admiration when I first saw it : I plainly saw such a sudden alteration in the face of nature, as gave me a most agreeable surprize, in sailing but two mile through the gulph.

Uppon the bay side is nothing to be seen but barren rocks, and parched vales ; no herbage, nor trees, nor shrubbs ; and the litle verdure there is, is so pauled and sickly, and tinctured with those rusty waters, as makes it offensive to look att. But here all is florid and green, the verdure so fresh and lively, the woods in such decorum and statelyness, as shew us those kindly vapours and effluvia they suck from the waters of this sea Artiwinipeck.

I remark that all along the coast down to Artiwinipeck, there is no regular tide, and that it is entirely under the goverment of the winds ; that litle languid motion it has setts to the northward. When we lay at the Decoy, we could perceive it rise and fall three or four inches alternately, as the wind blow'd fainter or fresher ; likewise, we found at Smiths Sound, at Hopwell Head, and at the gulph, it constantly set along shore to northward, and which was quicker near the capes, and more languid in the bays. We observed the tides had been considerably higher in all places at perticular times, which confirms me in opinion, that it is entirely under the influence of the winds ; and the luminaries have very litle or no effect on these tides, as I very carefully noted, when I observed them at full and change of the moon. And as we had fine wether the whole time, so the influx was in a manner insinsible ; and this I collected from many trials in all those places at the Decoy at Smith Sound, where the coast lyes with an inclining angle : there it swells higher by three or four foot, but at other places, near points or cape land, I never could perceive it rise above seventeen inches at Lady Lakes Grove, whereas at Richmond Fort it flowed four foot at spring tides. These places are but fourteen miles distant, which is entirely owing to the position of the coast, which compressis the fluid in motion, and causes it to swell above the ordinary levill. The same circumstance was also conspicuous at Coapache-un-e-sepee, where the waters are compressed, but not repulsed in their courses by the inclination of the shores; for in Groves Sound, nor at the cateracts, there was no appearance of this flux above seventeen or eighteen inches. And, therefore, I make no doubt, but at the coming on of those potent and powerfull northerly winds in the fall of the year which prevail in Hudsons Bay, that the flux may continue many hours; and so alternately when those blasts are over, it will require the like time to subside down to the ordinary levill.

The gulph in perticular is so diminutive and disproportionate to the size and capacity of Artiwinipeck, that it is no wonder that sea should be regardless of the influence of the luminaries. I should have been glad of a powerfull northwest wind while I lay at the Grove to have confirmed me in my conjecture; but during the summer heats, there can come no bleak cold winds over those barren, bare mountains, which acquire such a degree of heat as is hard to conceive, and which rarifie the air, and warm it, that they seldom reach the coast; I say during the summer months, but are turned off and reverberated by the extriordinary height and heat of those tremendious hills. These conjectures were confirmed in the year 1750; when a powerfull north-west wind blowed, it continued to flow forty-eight hours without intermission, and rose higher by two foot and two inches than I had remarked before; likewise, we had a storm at south-east, when the waters shrunk one foot and ten inches lower than I had seen before, so that at Richmond Fort, those two extreams are eight foot asunder, beyond which they seldom or ever stray; but, as was said, the ordinary tide their, is near four foot, and at the Grove, seventeen inches, as was said before.

If my conjecture holds good, it will suggest to us a probability of finding a more commodious passage down to
James's Bay, which, in all likelihood, is much sooner disin-
cumbred of ice, by those constant draining currents from the
lands, and the reflected winds which clears this coast and
expands the atmosphere. But the determination of this conjecture, and some others, must be left to futurity. I say, if
our ships could avoid those immense bodys of ice in going
down that bay (which makes that voyage always precarious),
it would give a security to that navigation and setlements as
would free them from many anxious concerns, which, as it
is, makes success doubtfull.

From Cape Diggs to Sir Thomas Smiths Sound, is a barren, plain coast, and foul ground four mile of into twenty
fatham, where you fall into an oazy bottam; from thence to
the Point of Portland the coast is a low fenny marsh, with
litle tufts here and there, but is so cover'd by banks and
broken ground, that there is no coming nearer than twenty
or twenty-five fatham.

Point of Portland is the northermost promontary of the
high lands, but is so covered with the Duble Dozens, that it
most remarkable for its heith than otherwise. From thence
to the Gulph of Hazard (called in Indian, Qua-qua-cheek-a-
wan), is a most bold coast, to be seen many leagues of att sea,
and cover'd by high, bold islands, which make a fine channile
between them and the main. Those to Hopwell Head are
so like one another in form, make, and size, that I dared not
make other distinction than Holms of Hopwell, least my
successors should cavill with me. But to southward of that
head, down to the gulph, are so remarkable one from another,
that I have not scrupled to assine names to all of them, and
distinguish them so to futurity, so necessary to make this
coast inteligable.

But all along that coast you have pretty deap water, untill
you come near the verge of those islands, where is foul

broken ground ; and from Solitary Islands to the Comittees, is a ridge from thirty-five to fifteen, which may hereafter be of good use when better known, which is not less than seven leagues from the main. As our boats went through the chaniles of Hopwell and Richmond, I am informed there is very good anchorage every where, and many fair sound and inlet through those chains of islands, and that nothing but a litle experience is wanting to make it the most commodious navigation in the world ; and I should think it no hard task for a small boat to go from Cape Diggs to Slude River.

We vizitted all the highest mountains in our progress, which overlooks that country to a great distance, but observed neither bush nor braque, but a sort of snow moss here and there in the declivities ; in the vales is a sort of rye grass, some snow-drops, vilet and white, without odour ; on the bare mountains it is not easie to conceive how they are heated, and I suspect this to be real cause why this country is quite forsaken during those heats, which warms the air to such a degree as banish the cold wether game from these parts, and so both beasts and men do ramble by necessity. If I conjecture right, the spring hunts will answer best ; for, altho we saw no living thing uppon the land or water, except what is befor taken notice of, yet we saw evident marks and traces of men and beasts and fowls in every place we toucht att all along the coast ; but is so barren, and the verdure so languid and sickly, the sudden change we met in passing through the gulph gave me a most agreeable surprise.

When I first entred the sea of Artiwinipeck, I was struck with the amazing grandour and beauty of the place, those asstonishing mountains which border the sound are so adorned with such beautifull verdure, and trees in such decorum and order, as if art had conspired with nature to make those tremendious hills more delightfull, where those rows of evergreens ascend stratum super stratum up to their

very summitts, form a most delightfull border, and down to
the very sea, to adorn and embellish that prodigious mountain.

On the right appears Lady Lakes Grove, under a stupend-
ous mountain, from whence fall a vissable cascade, which
throws itself in serpentine folds in many streams through
that grove into the sea, refreshing and enlivening all the
verdure near it.

Artiwinipeck, open to your view, presents you with an in-
closure of high mountains such as is not in the known world,
whose skirts and borders are so embellised with woods and
grass and plains, and interspersed with low islands here and
there, some covered with woods and grass and evergreens,
and others bare and barren at convenient distances, as make
a most delightfull landscape, and as if nature had been resolved to make the contrast inimitable.    And it is not easie
to conceive what an intense heat those barren bare rocks and
mountains acquire during the summer months (which are
natures hot beds), and which warms the air to such a degree
as setts all nature in a high ferment? and we our selves are
not a litle affected with those sultry blasts.

The sea contributes its part by affording plenty of water,
and is so indented with points and islands innumerable,
scattered here and there, as never to be boisterous nor dangerous, near which you have anchorage and anchor ground
every where.

The bottam is coverd with fine muscles, and sea-eggs, and
clamms, and spouts, and scallops, and other shell-fish, which
allures those shoals of fish you see come through the sound
every day, as well as those salmon, titimegg, and lake fish,
which abounds in every place within the gulph.    The seels
in the gulph are innumerable, and the fish-fowl covers the
waters uppon the influx, but rest and retire on the ebb.

The hunting grounds all show how well they are stockt at
proper seasons ; partridge and ducks always thus furnished

for the subsistance and recreation of fish, of fowl, of beasts, and men, we had some reason to expect to meet with the footsteps and traces of many tribes of Indians, which we did every where in our progress round that sea; and deer in herds, not only in those numberless declivities, but on all the islands we touched att.

In short, such is the beautifull situation of Lady Lakes Grove, the awfull grandure of Mount Eden, the delightfull groves of Grove Sound, the towring grotto and inchanting vine yard, and elegant situation of Richmond Fort, and the inimitable borders of Winters Mort Lake, as is not to be parrelled in Hudsons Bay, if in the whole world.

Thus much in justice I must need say, and recommend it to posterity, to add, to alter, and correct my faults and misrepresentations, improve my hints if they deserve it, confirm or controul my conjectures, and so they shall do an acceptable service to truth, to the company, and to mankind in general.[1]

As for the interior parts of the Labrodore, it is wholy occupied by the northern Indians before taken notice of, who live and depend mostly on fish and deers flesh; woolves, foxes, and otters, affords cloathing; and as these are to be had by traps, and ginns, and other contrivances, their necessities nor ambition dont prompt them to desire many things from us : our twine, fish-hooks, ice chizzels, ketles, and small wares, make up the ultimate of their wants. As for guns, powder, and shott, their are numbers of them dont know their use. The moulted fowls at proper seasons, and what else may be had with the bow and arrow, procure enough for change of dyett, who live in great plenty otherwise, do reduce these peoples wants into a narrow compass.

---

[1] It is evident from this observation, that these remarks were intended to be preserved to posterity ; and it must be admitted, that although a century has elapsed since they were written, they contain much interesting matter worthy of being preserved among the works of the Hakluyt Society.

The skirts and borders of Labrodore are hilly and mountainous on every side (a small part excepted); but the interior parts is covered with lakes and morassis to a wide extent, which affords an easy communication into all our principal rivers; but as above, these people have their food and rayment on so easy terms, that hardly one in twenty have ever taken the trouble to go to ours, or any of the French setlements. Indolence and idleness has a good share in this indifference: but surely tis a mark of great wisdom in them.

However, those few that has frequented the setlements, begin to like our commodities better; their women like our nicknacks and guegaws, and the men begin to love brandy, bread, and tobacco, so that a litle address and management will bring these happy drones out of this profound lethargy. You'll say these people would, from their manner of life, have increased faster than the other indians; but the reason I gave before has, in some measure, prevented them; and now it will be a good motive to apply themselves in earnest to the use and defence of the gun, who, by the aid and convenience of our setlement at Richmond Fort, will be enabled to keep in a body, and repell force by force, without being divided, or under a necessity to travell a great distance from their familys, by having all those things brought to their own doors.

All the hilly and mountanious parts of Labrodore are occupied by the Usquemews, from the bay of Saint Lawrence on the southern, eastern, and northern borders, and all along the east main to 56° and 57° latitude, and on all the islands adjacent, who are the seamen and fishermen on salt waters, as those are on inland lakes and fresh water rivers. Both one and other getts great quantities of deer; but whales, seels, and sea-horses, are the principle support of the Esquemews; wether these retreat and retire to any distance from the sea side uppon the approch of winter, or are wearid with

12

their long summer day, and creep into their winters cave to
rest, this is certain, we never saw but once or twice a single
Usquemew in many years experience in the homeward
bound passage, altho we have been detained by contrary
winds at all their haunts.

The interior parts of Labrodore affords good shelter, and
woods plenty for the northern Indians, who dress their
victuals as we do ; and dry'd fish supply the want of bread ;
they are very nasty in their persons, as all the Indians are ;
but not offensive in their filth, as the Esquemews.

I had a tribe in the year 1750 came of at the Deception,
very different from any I had seen before (except those at the
Four Usquemews), about sixty men, women, and chilldren,
of a swarthy Indian complection, all cloathed in deer skins,
bears and woalves, so alert and sprightly, not so fatt and
bloated as the Usquemews, nor so thin and megre as the
Indians ; I took them to be those very bordering northern
Indians we have before attempted to discribe, but it came
on blowing weather and prevented my making further remarks ; if I conjecture right, the allarums we gave last year
at Diggs, at the Four Esquemews, at Cape Smith, at the
Decoy, at Hopwell, and at the Dozens, had excited their
curiosity down to the sea side to be satisfied, for they
had nothing to trade but their breeches, of which I have a
sample.

What remains to be added to our geography, is a word
or two on the seasons proper to prosecute this navigation.
And as it is very hazardous to enter the streights before the
begining of July, for ice, so it is dangerous to be in that bay
after the middle of September ; the gales of wind and snow
setts in for a continuence, with very short calm intervals ;
the severe frost are such that you cannot work a ship ; possibly as the frost prevails the winds decrease, but to what
purpose ? when blocks are locks, and ropes are bolts, and
sails can neither be taken in nor left out, is surely the last

extremity ; the new ice near the shores and rivers, and the wash of the sea, stick to your ship and ropes like bird-lime, cand in your sails like pitch, and so all opperations by water ceasis, in the northern parts of the bay first, and so southward soon after : the winds on the land are variable, and you have short intervals of fine weather in the day time, untill the end of October ; but those violent gales of frost and snow are so frequent, that all our craft are put into winter quarters ; when the rivers are covered with ice, and the shores are lined to a great distance, and water disappeares, the land cloathed with snow, then prevales those violent piercing winds, which no creature can face for a continuence (except some short intervalls). And so apprehensive are our people of being caught out in those frightfull drifts at any distance from the factorys, that they never suffer a stranger to go a bow shott from the palisades without a person of experience with them.

Those terrible snow drifts and dark condensed foggs are hardly to be guarded against. Even the most experienced men we have, have been at times put to great extreamitys. Thus I have given you my sentiments on every part relating to this voyage ; your own prudence must supply whats wanting ; and as these remarks may be of pecullier use and service to you in your employment to and from that country, so it will be necessary for you to conceal these remarks from every other person. And I charge you to keep them secret, least others should draw consequences from them I never intended, to the prejudice of the Hudsons Bay Company. But if at any time hereafter the Company should reject you and spurn you from them, and deny you a moderate employment, in that case you are at liberty ; and it is my will and command that every part be made publick for the use and benefitt of mankind.

I have this to say, that no other person before my time ever collected so many notes, and but very few have had more experience nor better opportunities to explain this geography. The meanness and contemptable application I have drawn require some indulgence ; but the hydrographycall parts are so well adjusted, and with such care, that I do willingly submitt them to the test of time.

Thus I conclude, with my prayers, that God that he will give you a right use of them, and conclude,

YOUR AFFECTIONATE FATHER.

# APPENDAGE.

YORK Fort is 10ᶜ 45′ west longitude from the north end of Mansfeild; also 11° 15′ west longitude to the west main, in latitude 58° 00′ N.

It flowed in Ham Sound 9 hrs. 45′ on the full and change of the moon; but the tide run untill 10 hrs. 30′.

It flowes on the coast from Tod Head to Buckannes nearly 0 hrs. 45′, or S. by W. full and change, and runs half-tide.

Buchanness is in latitude 57° 25′ N.; variation, 14° 30′ north-westerly.

The course from Battery Head to South Ronalsa is N.N.W. twenty-five leagues; and this is confirmed by sundry experiments.

Cape Henrietta Maria is in longitude 84° 00′ W. from London, or 5° W. from Cape Diggs.

East Barrow Island is twelve mile to northward of Hoy Head, and seventy-eight ditto to westward of ditto.

Hoy Head is in latitude 58° 55′ N., and longitude 3° 30′ W. from London.

Stack I'le bears from Hoy Head W. ½ N. eleven leagues.

East Barrow to Hoy Head, E.S.E., twenty-six leagues.

Cape of Resolution to Nix Compestriss, cours N.W. by W. sixty-six miles, in latitude 62° 04′ N.

Observed in latitude 62° 20′ N., when Upper Savage I'le bore N. ½ E. five leagues; variation, 38ᶜ 30′ north-westerly.

From Cape Diggs to the north, and nearest part of Mansfeild, bears E. and W. fifty miles.

From Cape Diggs to the West Main, in latitude 60° 00′ N., is 16° W. longitude. Another note says Churchill River is 15° 20′ W. longitude to Cape Diggs.

From Cape Diggs to the west end of Cape Charles, is ninety miles east, and twenty-two miles northing.

From Cape Diggs to the Cape of Resolution, 14° 20′ E. longitude.

From the Cape of Resolution to Cape Farewell, 19° 20′ E. longitude. Confirmed, whose latitude is 59° 40′ N.

From C. Resolution to the East Barrow Island, 62° 25′ E. longitude.

From Cape Diggs to Carieswansnest, 6° 20′ W. longitude; ditto, to Cape Nesdrake, 5° 45′ west ditto; ditto, to the West Main, in latitude 59° 45′ N.; 15° 00′ W. longitude; which is a low, levill, barren land, and tolerable soundings in fifteen fath., four mile from the land.

Moulting Island, in latitude 59° 35′ N., one mile and a half from the shore, is thirteen leagues N.N.W. from Usquemow Point, and is remarkable.

Observed in latitude 62° 45′ N., when the north end of Mansfeild bore south five leagues; Diggs, E.S.E.; Nothingham, E. by N.; and run east forty mile, when Cape Diggs bore south five leagues.

From Cape Diggs to C. Resolution, 14° 02′ E. longitude, in seven days.

From the east end of Cape Charles to the east end of Salisbury Ile, is fifty-eight miles westing, whose latitude is 62° 42′ N.


### REMARKS IN SAILING INTO HAYS RIVER.

Bouy of the fair way uppon the flatts, bears from the beacon in Five Fatham Hole, N.E. by E. and S.W. by W., five mile, and lyes in ten foot water.

Bouy in that hole bears from the beacon N.N.E. ½ E. and

S.S.W. ½ W.; and from the bouy on the south point of Stones, N.E. ½ N. and S.W. ½ S.

Bouy of the south point of Stones, to the bouy of the Upper Hole, N.N.E. ½ E. and S.S.W. ½ W. That bouy lyes with the becons on the Marsh Shutt in one, and bears W. ½ S. and E. ½ N., in fifteen foot at low water.

I observed in latitude 58° 38′ N., near Port Nelson shoalds, 16° 00′ north-westerly; variation by sundry azimouths.

Ditto at Five Hole, latitude 57° 10′ N. Confirmed 1738, 40° longitude from Usquemow Point, 2° 20′ E.; but to round the shoalds, 2° 35′ E., in miles seventy-four or eighty-two ditto.

Stone River is sixteen miles from York Fort, and bears from Five Fatham Hole E.S.E. ½ S.

From Five Fatham Hole to Cape Diggs in eight days, 13° 42′ E. longitude.

From Cape Diggs to Carieswansnest, in 62° 15′ latitude, 7° 31′ W. longitude; from that low point the land trends N. by E.; five leagues off you have one hundred and twenty fatham.

I observed at York Fort the latitude, 57° 00′ N.; ditto, when Stone River bore S. ½ W. 57° 25′ N.; dist. five leagues in seven fatham.

N.B. Keep Hungry Bluff S.W. ½ S. The Point of Marsh, W. by S. is the best water; 'tis three miles from the factory to the beacons on the Point of Marsh, and it is two miles and ten yards athwart from high water mark to ditto at the factory.

### REMARKS ON THE TIDES ADJACENT TO THE CAPE SOUTHAMPTON COAST AND ELSWERE.

In latitude 62° 15′, longitude 5° 46′ W. from Diggs, in forty-six fatham, mud at 10 A.M., a slack.

Four leagues from land, in forty-five fatham, mud at 7 P.M., it set one mile and eight-tenths E. by S. ½ S.

In latitude 61° 56′ N., 7° 13′ W. from Diggs, it set at 1 P.M., seven-tenths of a mile N.W.; in one hundred and twenty fatham, soft ground, Carieswansnest north six leagues.

At 2 P.M. it sett four-tenths of a mile E. by S.; latitude, 60° 48′ N.

At 5 P.M. a slack; longitude, 13° 29′ W. from Cape Diggs.

At 8 P.M. it sett five-tenths of a mile W. by N., in seventy-six to seventy fatham, ouzy.

At 8 A.M. we had a slack; latitude, 61° 51′ N.

At 12, noon, it sett six-tenths of a mile S.S.E.; longitude, 16° 00′ W. from C. Diggs.

At 2 P.M. it sett four-tenths of a mile N.N.W. At anchor near Whale Cove, in twelve fatham water, hard ground, fifteen islands in sight.

At 2 P.M. it sett six-tenths of a mile W. by N. ½ N.; latitude, 61° 30′ N.

At 5 P.M. it sett four-tenths of a mile N.E. by N.; longitude, 15° 46′ W. from Diggs.

At 9 P.M. it sett four-tenths of a mile N.E., in forty-two to forty-five fatham water.

From Five Fatham Hole to the east end of Notingham Island in five days, 14° 46′ E. longitude.

I observed in latitude 58° 42′ N., when Flannil Islands bore S. by E. six leagues distance.

I sett the north end of Lewis Island bore S.W. by S. about seven leagues; East Barrow, N. by E. ⅓ E. five leagues; the West Barrow, N. by W.; and are three mile asunder. Lewis Island, on the north end, is prett levell and cliffy; the south part, mountainous and hilly.

East Barrow Island is in latitude 59° 05′ N. and longitude east from Resolution, 55° 12′ E.

I observed in latitude 58° 43′ N., when Pictland Skerrys bore W. by N., and the south end of Ronalsa bore N. by W. six leagues.

By another account, Girdleness is thirty-seven miles to eastward of Holm Sound.

I stood of five miles from Mockbegger into twenty fatham, and tacked when Haisbrough Sand bore east twelve mile.

Flambrough Head in latitude 54° 05′ N.; in steering north it carryed us twenty-one mile to eastward of Buchanness. By this account, it is longitude 1° 56′ W. from London, and its latitude 57° 35′ N.

Stock and Skerry in one bears N.E. by E. four miles asunder.

From London to Resolution made 64° 30′ W. longitude.

I observed in latitude 61° 21′ N., when Cape Warwick bore N.W. by W.

I observed in latitude 62° 10′ N., when the Middle Salvage bore E. ½ S. five leagues.

I observed in latitude 62° 26′ N., when Salvage Point bore N. by E. ⅛ E. four leagues.

I observed in latitude 62° 59′ N., when east end of Salisbury bore N.E. by E.; west end of ditto bore N.E. by N.; east end of Notingham, N. ½ E.; west end of ditto, N. ½ W.; Cape Walsingham, W.

All well defined.

N.W. from Cape Henrietta Maria you have broken ground from five and a half to eleven fatham, in those depths we steered, untill the Cape bore south six miles, when we dropt into ten, twelve, fourteen fatham oaz.

I observed in latitude 55 15′ N., when the Cape bore W. by N. seven miles; longitude, 4° W. from Cape Diggs.

From Cape Henrietta Maria to latitude 53° 16′ N., and eighty-one miles to eastward, I set the North Twinn from E. by S. to E. by N. ½ N. seven leagues; Viners Island from S.W. by W. to W. by N. about five leagues.

When the east end of Agomisco bore S.W., the east end of the North Twinn bore E.N.E.

I went from the ship in Moose River Road, and rowed

into the mouth of that river as follows : North Bluff,W.N.W.
at 6 hrs. 27', past the outer bouy in four fathams ; 6 hrs. 56'
past the second bouy, three and three quarters fathams ;
6 hrs. 58' past the third bouy, three and a quarter fathams ;
7 hrs..08' ditto fourth bouy in three fathams ; 7 hrs. 15' ditto
fifth bouy, three, one foot less ; 7 hrs. 22' ditto sixth bouy,
two and a half fatham ; becons, two and a half fathams.

We returned on board by 9 h. 47', and rowed four mile
an hour.

At the North Sand Beacon, three and a quarter fatham
best water ; second ditto, three ditto ; third ditto, three and
a quarter ditto ; fourth ditto, three ditto ; fifth ditto, three
and a quarter ditto ; sixth ditto, three and a half ditto,
becon ; seventh ditto, four and a half ditto, bouy at Ship-
hole.

From the bouy in Moose River Road 'tis six miles to the
North Point ; twenty-one miles N.N.W. $\frac{1}{2}$ W. to Wapisco ;
nineteen miles N.W. by N. to Cockishpenny ; twenty-
four miles N.W. by W. to the bouy of the Fairway, at the
entrance of Albany River. By keeping in five fatham is a
surer way to find the bouy.

I observed in latitude 51° 40' N., when the bouy bore
S.S.W. two miles ; North Bluff, W.N.W. six miles. I came
out uppon a neap tide. The bar begins half a mile without
the Sand Heads, and is one mile in breadth ; we had not less
than fourteen and a half foot. N.B.—As a memento, when
the Sand Heads are covered, you have above twelve foot
uppon the bar.

The south end of Mansfeild, in latitude 61° 40' N. lyes
uppon the meridian of the North Bear ; the West Sleeper, in
latitude 59° 50' N., is sixteen miles to westward.

From Moose River Road to the Gaskitt, fifty-eight miles
northe ; from thence to the South Bear, fifty miles westing ;
and 2° 00' E. longitude from thence to Cape Diggs. And by
computing your time at five miles a day, it will pritty nearly

account for that easterly current you have from C. H. Maria to Mansfeild.

From Buttons Iles to Silly in twenty-two days, 59° 30′ E. longitude.

From Rattery Head to Holm Sound, N. by W., twenty-five leagues.

From London to Resolution, 63° 50′ E. longitude, in latitude 61° 40′ N., where is a litle island five miles from the East Bluff, Shut in bear, N. by E. By another account, 63° 30′ E. longitude.

Cape Usquemow, in latitude 61° 10′ N., longitude 16° 40′ W. from Cape Diggs, appears like Knights Hill near Cape Churchill : make in a point, and you have broken ground, which distracts the tides and turns them in eddies and over-falls. We had thirty-five, twenty, thirty, twenty-five, twenty-seven, twenty-five ; black peper, mixt with yellow shells, hard ground. Cape, N.N.W. five leagues.

Cape Pembroke, in latitude 63° 05′ N., fifty-seven miles east to the north end of Mansfeild ; seventy-six miles east to Cape Walsingham ; eighteen miles to the east end of Salisbury ; and our crs. was E. ¼ N. one hundred and forty-nine miles to the west end of Cape Charles : all in twenty-four hours.

From Cape Diggs to Resolution, 14° 18′ E. longitude.

From Resolution to the East Barrow, 62° 20′ E.

I observed, in latitude 58° 47′ N., when it bore N.N.W. seven leagues.

Europa Point-on-Lewis, W.S.W. nine leagues.

Cape Wrath, S.S.E. nine leagues, we run in sight of Lewis Island twenty leagues : the southermost parts are very high land, but the north end is pritty levill.

From Resolution to Hoy Head, 64° 30′ E. longitude.

All remarks to Resolution confirmed.

I made but 58° W. longitude from Hoy Head to Resolution ; but when you compute the errors in latitude southerly, in twenty-one days passage, in a current nearly S.W., four and a half mile a day westing, this being digested in the log, I am perswaded it will reconcile the outward and homward bound journalls.

I have named east end of the north shore above Lower Savage I'les, the East Bluff, fifteen leagues, above three mile from Sadle Back.   I observ'd in latitude 62° 06' N.

I observed the south end of Mansfeild in 61° 40' N.; tis a low point of banks of shells.   On the east side, forty fatham is near enough; but on the south and west, 'tis flatt of a pritty distance.

From Litle Agomisco, we run in five and a half to six and a half fatham S.E. by E.   Observ'd in latitude 53° 29 N.; nearest dis. S.S.W. six miles.

We sailed from the north-east Horn of Agomisco S. by E., and got in three miles to westward of the Gaskitt.   I am of oppinion their is a wide chanile to westward : their is a ridge from it two mile to northward, and it spits of half a mile to southward from a dry bank of shingle a quarter of a mile long.

From Tutherly Island I stood twenty mile W.S.W., and tackt one mile from the Gaskitt.   This narrow is twenty-one miles wide ; 'tis thirty-two miles to eastward of Albany Road, where I lay twelve mile east from the North Sand Head, and 'tis fifty-seven miles to eastward of the South Bear, and that island is fourteen miles to westward of the North Sand Head.

I observed the north end of Mansfeild in 62° 30' N. latitude on the meridian of the Bears.   The westermost of Bakers Dozen is four mile to westward of that meridian, in latitude 58° 20' N.

Flambrough Head, in latitude 54° 08' N. longitude, 0° 11' E. from London.

I observed, in latitude 61° 35' N., when the East Bluff of Resolution bore N.W. by N. five leagues, Cape Warwick

W. by N. ½ N. eight leagues, and made home to the land 60° 54 E. from Hoy Head.

South part of Notingham is in latitude 63° 15′ N.

South end of Mansfeild in latitude 61° 40′ N.

We saw the Bear Islands in twenty-five fatham oaz south, do. east four leagues; we steered S. by E. eighty-eight miles; south, seven miles, in depths twenty-nine, sixteen, twenty, twenty-three, to the East Horn of Agomisco, west one mile, to nine, eleven, twelve, fifteen, sixteen, twenty; and going fourteen miles further S. by E., run into thirty fath., the water of a gall coulour. The Bear Islands, by this acct., is 3° 00′ W. from Cape Diggs.

I observed in latitude 52° 32′ N., half a mile from the Gaskitt, this bank and ridge is two miles in length from north to south; the dry part is nearest the south end; we had ten to fifteen fatham within half a mile; and this shoald lyes fourteen miles to eastward of the Horn of Agomisco.

This East Wash, or Horn of Agomisco, is thirty-four miles to eastward of the Bear Islands, in latitude 53° 00′ N.: it is by this note fourteen miles to westward of the Gaskitt, in latitude 52° 32′ N.; the South Bear in latitude 54° 28′ N. from hence, crs. and dist.

I observed in latitude 51° 34′ N., when the North Point bore W.N.W. ½ N., Robersons Island, S.S.W.; bouy of the Fair Way, S.W. by S. one mile; the Bluffs at Wa-waes Creeks, W. by N., in four and a half fatham at anchor: the Gaskitt from this buoy bears N. by E. fifty-six miles.

The channile into this river is thus: from the Sand Heads you steer N.N.E. one and a half mile, from eleven and a half foot to nine at low water; then N.E. one and a half mile, nine, nine, nine foot over the barr into eleven, twelve, fourteen, fifteen foot; go one mile further to the Fair Way buoy, which I compute is near six miles into Sand Heads beacons. The coast has many bank, and lyes of into five fatham and broken ground; and the two bouys of the Fair Way at Moose

River and Albany River is sixty-four mile on three courses distant.

From Albany Road, ten miles east from the North Sand Head, we steered E. ⅓ N. thirty-two miles to the Gaskitt, in latitude 52° 33′ N. ; from thence, N. by W. ¾ W., thirty-nine miles to the Horn of Agomisco, in nine and a half fath. water, when it was W. by S. two miles, in latitude 53° 04′ N. The true bearings from these two dangerous shoald is nearly S.S.E. and N.N.W. thirty-seven miles ; from hence, N.N.W. ¼ W., into 54° 08′ N. latitude, we came to a rock caled Flotars Wash, which bears from the South Bear W. 40° ; southerly, sixteen miles.

I observed the North Bear in latitude 54° 32′ N.

I observed the Bakers Dozen, fourteen in number, in latitude 59° 05′ N., from S.E. to N.E. by E., nearest dist. four leagues. By this acct. uppon the meridian of the North Bear, in 2° 50′ W. longitude from Cape Diggs, the southeast pt. of Mansfeild is 1° 00′ E. longitude from the said meridian.

St. Kilday Islands are five in number ; the westermost is like a sugar loaff in form. We had seventy-five fatham, N.E., five leagues from them. We run eight leagues N E. by E. to the Flannin Iles, and made longitude 60° 43′ E. from Buttons I'les to Hoy Head.

By this note, the north part of Lewis Island is a levill champaine land, but the south part is very high and mountainous, and seldom uncover'd of clouds. Near Cape Wrath, S.W. from Hoy Head, are two round mountains ; and more to eastward are another prodigious one, which appears, in points and summits, like the teeth of a saw : the latitude of this cape is nearly 58° 35′ N.

I observed Salvage Point in latitude 62° 16′ N.

The South Bear is forty-seven miles to westward and eighty-three miles to northward of the Horn of Agomisco.

The Lower Hole in Moos River is one third of a mile

W. $\frac{1}{2}$ N. from the South Sand beacon, thirteen foot at low water: we came over the bar in twelve foot water, and run sixty-four miles from this road to Albany Road.

You are not to stand above sixteen miles athwart from Agomisco towards the North Twinn. It is nearly thirty miles from the two lands; but the shoalds of one, and a ridge of rocks from the other, require fourteen miles for birth. I tackt in twenty-nine fatham, when the North Twinn bore from E. $\frac{1}{2}$ S. to N.E. $\frac{1}{2}$ E., dist. ten miles; and this island strechis N.N.E. twelve miles in lenth. I observed the latitude in 53° 20′ N., and stood sixteen miles back to the Horn of Agomisco, one mile W. by N.

I observed the West Sleeper in latitude 59° 40′ N. By this note it is five leagues to westward of the North Bear; and this North Bear is 2° 26′ W. longitude from Cape Diggs.

From Resolution to St. Kilday in fourteen days, we made 58° 03′ E. longitude; Cape Farewell, 19° 20′ E. from the Dipt. St. Kilday bore S. by W. twelve leagues. Observed in latitude 58° 35′ N.

From Roseness to Tinmouth Castle, S. by E. seventy-seven miles, and south one hundred and sixty miles, when the latter bore W. by S. seven leagues in thirty-six hours.

From Hoy Head to Resolution in twenty-four days, 61° 54′ W. longitud.

Gulph Hazard is 2° 10′ E. from Cape Diggs; homeward, 2° 01′ E.; latitude, 56° 22′ N.; variation, 29° north-westerly. It flows eleven o'clock full, and change and risis but seventeen inches at the gulph at an ordinary tide.

From Resolution to the Lizard in twenty-five days, 62° 00′ E. longitude.

From Rattery Head to Roseness, N. by W. $\frac{1}{2}$ W., eighty-one miles in sixteen hours.

I observed Hoy Head in latitude 58° 52′ N.

Near the Labrodore, in latitude 60° 20′ N., 58° W. from

London, we had a current sett to southward eighteen miles in one day.

At Cove Harbour, in the middle Salvage Isles, it flowed ten hrs. 20′ on the full and change, and rise twenty-five foot nine inches; but on the 3d after full, with a strong S.E. wind, it rise twenty-nine foot.

I observed Cape Smith in latitude 60° 56′ N., longitude 1° 48′ W. from Cape Diggs, or twenty-two miles. You have a current three mile north a day.

At Richmond Road in Artiwinipeck, the tide risis three foot four and a half inch at an ordinary tide; in a storm at N.W., it rises seven foot, increasing for forty-eight hours; it shrunk on the contrary wind for the like time.

Bonds Inlet is six miles long, and four miles wide in the narrowest part, W.S.W. ½ S. seven leagues through all the islands.

St. Kilday is one hundred and thirty miles to westward of Hoy Head.

From Resolution to Hoy Head, 61° 45′ E. longitude.

From London to Resolution, 62° 01′ W. longitude.

I observed the sun rise twelve minutes of time sooner then by calcullation in Hudsons Streights.

By this note, the south end of Mansfeild is in latitude 61° 38′ N.

I observed in latitude 60 13′ N., the North Sleeper, S.E. by E. four leagues, and the West Sleeper, S.S.W. ½ W. five leagues the latitude by this note.

N. Sleeper, 60° 04′ N.
W. Sleeper, 60° 00′ N. } longitude. { 2° 15′
1° 34′ } W. from C. Diggs.

By two curious observations to this purpose, I found, in sailing from Albany Road to the North Twinn, a north-east current twelve mile a day.

From Resolution to Cape Desolation in 61° 00′ N. latitude, the longitude 14° 36′ E.; Cape Farewell in 60° 20′ N. latitude; N. ¼ E. twelve leagues. We afterwards made the East

Barrow, 45° 44' E. longitude from this place ; but this note is imperfect.

I observed Flambrough Head 3° 37' E. longitude from Holm Sound. I observed the latitude in Albany Road, when the beacon on the North Sand Head bore W.S.W. eight miles, deducting a proportion of the dayly difference, 52° 20' N.

Gulph Hazard in latitude 56° 22' N.; longitude, 77° 00' W. from London.

1744. Observed St. Kilday is in latitude 58° 10' N.; longitude, 5° 30' W. from Hoy Head, four in number. Confirmed.

1745. From Resolution to Hoy Head, 61° 30' E. longitude.

I observed in latitude 61° 21' N., when Cape Warwick bore N.W. ½ N., and the last Bluff of Resolution north.

It flowed in Bonds Inlet two days after full moon, 12 o'clock, and rose fourteen foot; its latitude 62° 38' N., very deap water. In it there is a small rock on the north side ; as you enter from the streights, a strong tide ; and you have a small cove on the Cape side, which lyes open to the north-east.

Flatts of Hays River is eight miles over from Five Fath. Hole into six fatham cours, E.N.E. ½ N., into latitude 57° 28' N.

When the first Bluff to westward of Knights Hill bears S. ½ E., you go of those shoalds from seven fatham, sixteen and seventeen fatham, and soft ground ; where Usquemow Point bears W.S.W. ½ S. six leagues.

In latitude 61° 37' N., we saw the south end of Mansfeild N.W. by W. four leagues, which 13° 0' E. from Five Fatham Hole, and 14° 11' E. to Cape Diggs.

I observed Rokel in latitude 57° 38' N., 53° 24' E. longitude from Resolution, a solitary rock-like pyramid, and no ground one mile west from it, eighty fatham of line.

1744. East Barrow is two hundred and fifty-five miles to eastward of Rokel.

I observed in latitude 58° 49' N.: the East Barrow bore north six leagues ; the Butt of Lewis and East Barrow bears N.E. by N. and S.W. by S. sixteen leagues distant.

14

I observed the latitude 57° 34' N., when Rattery Head bore N.W. by N. four leagues.

I observed in latitude 61° 41' N., when the east bluff of Resolution W. by N. ½ N. six leagues.

In Ship Hole, in Moose River, I observed the latitude, 51° 26' N.; North Point, north seven or eight miles. It flowed seven hours and a half on the quarter day; so that S. ½ W. moon makes full sea.

Albany Road, in five fatham, is twenty-one miles east from the fort on Bailys Island.

The North Bear is 2° 30' W. longitude from Cape Diggs; and Mansfeild, on the south-east part, is six mile to eastward of that meridian.

From Resolution to St. Killday, 57° 33' E. longitude, in latitude 58° 10', four in number.

1747. From London to Resolution, 64° 30' W. longitude.

Cape Henrietta Maria is forty-nine miles to westward of the North Bear. By this note the South Bear is 2° 20' W. from Cape Diggs.

Observed a current of eight mile a day sett to southward in sailing down the streights, but 'tis much more near the south shore.

Gulph Hazard is caled, in Indian, Quaquachichchiwan, or, it swallows quickly.   Isbister.

1748. From Button Iles to St. Kilday in twelve day, 60° E. longitude; from ditto to Hoy Head, 63° 38' E. longitude.

In eighteen days that year run from Churchill River to Orkney.

I observed the latitude in Ice Cove, 62° 24' N.; ditto in Moose River Road, 51° 33' N.; North Bluff, W. ½ N. in four and a half fatham.

Teas Bay in latitude 54° 40' N.; longitude, 1° 30' W. from London.   Hoy Head, latitude 58° 52' N.; longitude, 4° 20' W. from London.

THE END.

# APPENDIX.

CAPTAIN MIDDLETON'S VOYAGE TO HUDSON'S BAY

FOR THE

DISCOVERY OF A NORTH-WEST PASSAGE,

(1741-42),

IN COMMAND OF THE "FURNACE" BOMB, AND "DISCOVERY" PINK ;
THE LATTER IN CHARGE OF MR. WM. MOOR.

# APPENDIX.

" 1741 (*Friday, July* 31). This day a council was held on board, in latitude 61° 02', longitude 86° 11' W.

" The question was put, and taken into consideration, whether it would be proper to proceed upon a discovery of a passage from Hudson's Bay to the South Sea directly; or to repair, with His Majesty's ships *Furnace* and *Discovery*, to Churchill River in Hudson's Bay, as the season of the year is too far advanced to proceed any farther, and there being a necessity of securing the vessels, and providing necessaries for wintering as soon as possible : and it was unanimously resolved, considering the rigor of the winter in these parts of the world, the want of everything necessary for building lodgings for the men, a convenient place for securing the vessels from the dangers of the ice, the necessity of digging store-rooms for the provisions,—no brandy, spirits, nor strong beer being proof against the severity of the winter above ground,—the uncertainty of securing the vessels after the frost comes on, which usually happens in the beginning of September ; and the obstructions we may probably meet with in our passage, by fogs, calms, ice, and contrary winds.

" That it would be the best and surest method for the ser-

---

[1] From the original log of Captain Middleton, in the Record Office of the Admiralty.

vice in general, to proceed directly for Churchill River in
Hudson's Bay, there to secure His Majesty's vessels *Furnace*
and *Discovery*, with their provisions, stores, and ammunition;
and to provide convenient winter-quarters, firing, and necessary clothing, for their respective companies; and to wait
the breaking up of the ice next year, and then to attempt
the discovery of a passage from Hudson's Bay to the South
Sea.

"1741 (*Friday, 4th Sept.*): *at the mouth of our wintering
cove, Churchill River.*  Cold weather, with sleet and snow; the
winds variable.  Continued our men at work as above; every
tide, as we dig down, we meet with rocks and stones, which
we are obliged to blow up.  We got our anchors above high-
water mark.  Yesterday morning, as I was going forwards,
and the men running round with the capstan, I was jammed
between the end of one of the bars and the companion, which
took my breast and back bone, so that I fell down senseless
for some time; and when recovered a little, was in great
pain, and difficulty of breathing, but don't find any damage
inwardly.  I hope I shall, in a short time, recover again,
through the assistance of Providence.

"(*Sunday, 11th Oct.*) Clear air; cold weather.  This being
the anniversary of His Majesty's coronation day, we solemnized it in a particular manner.  We marched all our men
from the New Fort, under arms, to the cove where the ships
lay, being above two miles distant, and at noon discharged
twenty-eight guns, belonging to both ships, that were laid in
order on the shore for that purpose, where the two ships
winter.  The officers drank to His Majesty's health, and
success to the British arms, as the guns were firing.  It was
observed at the same time that the wine with which the
officers drank the aforesaid healths, and which was good port
wine, froze in the glass as soon as poured out of the bottle.
They marched back in the same order, with drums beating

and colours flying. When they arrived at the New Fort, they were drawn up in the middle of the area, where they went through their exercise, fired several vollies, and drank to the health of His Majesty, the Prince and Princess of Wales, and all the royal family. The Articles of War and Orders of the Navy were read to them. In the evening, His Majesty's officers, and those of the Hudson's Bay Company, were plentifully regaled ; and the men belonging to both ships, and the factory men, had thirty gallons of brandy made into punch, to drink the aforesaid healths, to which the natives were invited ; and the evening concluded with all possible demonstrations of joy, to the great pleasure and satisfaction of the natives.

" (*Tuesday, 13th Oct.*) Moderate warm weather ; much snow fell last night ; the wind variable. All the ice that lined the shores, without, and for two miles up the river, drove out of sight to sea ; the rest fast froze. People have crossed the river upon the ice, eight miles up, four days ago. I observe how so much ice is made in the bay, straits, and shores, in these parts ; and why there is more made some years than others. It is caused in the fall of the year, before the rivers, bays, and inlets, are froze fast ; for the ice that is made on the several lee shores increases at a great rate, near one mile in twenty-four hours, which at the flux and reflux of the tides breaks off, and when the wind blows from the shore is all carried out to sea, where it fastens together, and more increases with it. And as we find in the straits and bay greater quantities of ice some years than others, it is owing to the length of time these several rivers, inlets, bays, etc., are freezing fast ; for the sea is not, nor can freeze, without something to fasten upon. And if the rivers should keep open until the latter end of October, it would go near to fill Hudson's Bay one quarter full of ice. Now all the ice that's drove into the open bay, let the wind blow from any part of the compass, will have one side of it a weather side, which

makes a great increase by the wash of the sea against it; and
as the winter continues for nine months, there must be great
quantities made in that time."

It would appear from some of the following extracts, that
a liberal allowance of grog was issued to the men during
their sojourn in winter quarters, and which, doubtless, must
have been very prejudicial to their health; as the results, in
fact, proved, from the number of men who died.

"(*Friday, Oct. 30th*): *Churchill Fort*. Fresh gales and
clear weather; freezing very hard. This being the anniversary of His Majesty's birth day, we solemnized it in the same
manner we did the coronation, firing seventeen guns; the
tender, eleven. Drank to His Majesty's health and the royal
family, and distributed thirty gallons of brandy made into
punch, together with strong beer, among our people, the
factory's men, and natives, as before on the coronation day.

"(*Thursday, 5th Nov.*) Hard gales, with much snow, and
freezing. This being the anniversary of Gunpowder Treason,
and our guns being covered with snow, we played off some
fireworks at the New Fort, and gave our men and officers
thirty gallons of brandy and sugar to make punch, as before.

"(*Tuesday, 22nd Dec.*) Moderate gales, but very sharp air.
Most of the factory men and Indians that were hunting and
fishing for the ships' companies and the factory, are returned
here to keep their Christmas, according to custom, for twelve
or fourteen days. We shall give our people strong beer and
brandy every day all the time.

"(*Thursday, 24th Dec.*) Most of our people at the old
factory are very well, excepting two or three that are afflicted
with the scurvy, and were ailing before they came on shore
in this place. I have given them, ever since our English
beer has been expended, spruce beer and brandy, the only
means used here to prevent the scurvy."

A little further on it will be seen that it had not the effect, and many of the men were attacked with this frightful malady.

"1742 (*Saturday, 2nd January*). A hard gale all night, and drifting snow ; very cold, freezing every thing in my cabin, though a fire kept in from five in the morning till nine at night ; and when the fire is out, a red hot shot, twenty-four pounds' weight, hung up at the window to thaw it ; on the outside there are shutters to every window, six inches thick ; four large fires made in the stoves every day—a cart-load of wood for each ; yet all this will not keep things from freezing within doors.

"(*Monday, 4th Jan.*) Fair and clear weather, but extreme cold. I went out this forenoon with a design to take a walk ; but had not gone two hundred yards before my face was froze all over in a blister, so was obliged to return.

"(*Thursday, 4th Feb.*) This evening our surgeon came down from the old factory, after cutting off the men's toes, and the flesh of several that were froze and mortified. There are four men at the old factory very bad with the scurvy, twelve at the new factory very ill with the scurvy, the country distemper, and froze ; twenty-five at both places, belonging to both ships, not able to go abroad ; and seve-ral not able to help themselves. I get fresh provisions for those in the scurvy ; and the surgeon uses all possible means to save them. In the spring of the year we shall supply them with green herbs—the best remedy known here for the scurvy."

The supply of green herbs was certainly more likely to be efficacious than the " thirty gallons of brandy to make into punch."

"(*Saturday, 13th March*): *Churchill River.* Abraham
15

Page departed this life, after a long illness with a fever and scurvy; a very stout, able-bodied man, and a good seaman. We have, at this time, fifteen or sixteen very ill; several of them cannot live long. So extreme cold, there is no stirring abroad.

"(*Monday, 22nd March.*) Fair and moderate weather; in the morning, calm; at noon, veered to south-east. John Blair, an able seaman, died last night of the scurvy, after a long illness. Fourteen or fifteen more continue very ill of the same distemper. We continue serving them with fresh provisions and strong beer: those that are well are served with half brandy and half spruce beer; and a bottle of brandy and sugar to every four men, once a week, over and above their allowance.[1]

"(*Friday, 26th March.*) Henry Spencer died of the scurvy, being long ill. Most of them are carried off with a looseness.

"(*Monday, July 12th.*) Latitude, 65° 30'; longitude, 85° 55' W. Wind, weather, etc., as per log. Our way made, allowing for working among the ice, is N. 11 W., dist. twenty-one miles; depart., four miles: therefore latitude and longitude as above. At noon, a fair point, cape, or headland, appeared on the north shore, to the northward of Whale Bone Point, which bore from us eight or nine leagues, as above, in latitude 65° 10' N., and longitude from London, by accot., 86° 06' W., which I shall name Cape Dobbs. And now we are standing in for an inlet or strait, which makes a fair opening north-west from us, though not very wide, to secure our ships from the continual danger they must be exposed to by lying in the Welcome, or proceeding any further until the ice is gone; and if this cannot be done, we must forthwith return.

---

[1] This superabundant supply of spirits must have been most injurious to the men, who seem to have suffered severely, forming a great contrast to Captain Austin's and Captain Penny's ships during the winter of 1850-1.

"(*Tuesday, July* 13): *in the River Wager, North America.*
The weather, wind, and other remarks, as per log. Soundings and depths of water as below. At six, entering the
inlet, which was now suspected to be a river. Very good
soundings, no less than sixteen fathoms; and most of the
way, as we go up, twenty, thirty, and forty-four fathoms. It
was just low water as we entered. The tide runs five or six
miles an hour. This river, which I choose to name Wager
River, in honour of Sir Charles Wager (first Lord Commis-
sioner of the Admiralty), at four or five miles within its
entrance, is six or eight miles wide; four or five leagues up,
it is four or five leagues wide. There are several islands in
the middle, and some rocks, which we happily escaped. At
high water, the land on both sides as high as any in England.
About six leagues up, at our first anchoring, the tide runs
not above two miles an hour. At ten in the morning sent
the master with the boat to help the tender into anchor by
us, out of the tides and ice; but she is driven down with the
ebb again, it being calm, and thick ice surrounding her.

"(*Thursday, July* 15*th*.) Many of our men are very bad
of their old disease, the scurvy. Those who were on the
recovery when we came from Churchill, are grown worse
again; so that one half of them are unserviceable.

"(*Tuesday, July* 20*th*.) I returned on board, and brought
the deer, as above. Gave part to the tender, and the rest to
our sick people gratis, or over and above their allowance.
It was very strange, that, in this sickness, even a day or two
before they died, they would eat their whole allowance, and
a great deal more if they could get it.

"(*Sunday, August* 8*th*.) Latitude, 65°41'; longitude, 85°22'.
Wind, weather, etc., as above. Our course made since two
in the morning that we bore away, to noon, is S. 30 W.;
dist., forty-seven miles; depart., two hundred and thirty-five
miles. I returned on board last night, as above, having been
fifteen miles from the place where we landed. My clerk,

the carpenter, gunner, and one Indian, were with me. We passed over high mountains till we came to the furthermost, which overlooks the Frozen Strait, and the east bay on the other side, and could see the passage where the flood came in. The narrowest part of this strait is four or five leagues, being six or seven at the broadest, almost full of long small islands; its length is about sixteen or eighteen leagues. It stretches south-east round to the south. To the westward we could see it from beginning to end, all full of ice not yet broken up, quite fast to both shores and to the small islands. We saw very high land fifteen or twenty leagues to the southward of our station, which I take to run towards Cape Comfort, being the furthest that Bylot went; and the bay which Fox named Lord Weston's Portland, in part of Hudson's North Bay, about north-west from the west end of Nottingham, by comparing our longitude made with Fox's and Bylott's. As this last-mentioned bay and strait is quite full of ice not likely to be thawed this year, at least till very late, so as to allow time for a discovery, it was resolved in council to make the best of our way into Hudson's Bay homewards.

"(*Sunday*, 15*th Aug.*)  Latitude, 61° 25'; longitude, 92° 25'. I find I can do no more to the purpose I am ordered upon, and my men are most of them very much distempered; so that, by consultation, we find the best method to bear away for England."

*Letters[1] from Captain Middleton, commanding the Expedition for the Discovery of a North-West Passage through Hudson's Strait ; dated from their Winter Quarters in Churchill River, 28th June 1742, and addressed to Sir Charles Wager, First Lord of the Admiralty.*

" RIGHT HONBLE. SIR,—

" The last that I wrote to you from the Isles of Orkney was dated June the 25th, 1741. On the 27th I sailed from thence, the tender in company. The first and second day after we were out, had calms and contrary winds ; spoke with two ships, the one from New England, the other from Virginia,—both bound to London. After that, had favourable winds and weather. On the 16th of July made Cape Farewell, the east entrance of Davis's Straits, being very high, ragged land, covered with snow. It is in the latitude of 59° 45′ N., and longitude, from the meridian of London, about 46° W. ; which meridian I shall account my longitude from the rest of the voyage.

" On the 21st saw several large isles of ice in latitude 60° 30′, and longitude 61° 00′ W. On the 25th, made the south part of Cape Resolution, the north entrance of Hudson's Straits, being in the latitude of 61° 25′ N., and longitude, 64° 00′ W. At the same time sailed into the straits with a fair wind, but thick fog. The variation of the compass in this strait, is N. 40° westerly. Very strong and dangerous tides run in here, with overfalls, ripplings, and whirlings, yet very deep water,—two hundred fathom not far from the shore. The tides flow on change days E.S.E. and W.N.W. in the harbours on shore, and five fathom ; the flood comes from the eastward, and thither it returns.

" The 29th, got the length of Cape Diggs on the south side and west end of the straits, in latitude 62° 50′ N., and longi-

---

[1] The following letters are copied from the originals, in the Record Office of the Admiralty, and have never before been published.

tude 78° W., about one hundred and forty leagues from Cape
Resolution, which is the length of these straits. Found our
passage very clear of ice, only large isles that are for ever
seen on the coasts here. The land on both sides is very
high. The north side appears to be nothing but islands and
broken land, covered all the year with snow and pestered
with ice, unpassable excepting three months in the year.
The same evening we passed by the north end of Mansel's
Island, which is distant from Cape Diggs fourteen leagues,
and is in length twenty leagues, though in most places not
above three leagues broad; very low and dangerous coming
near it in the night and foggy weather, being deep water
close to, and cannot be seen above three or four miles from
the deck in clear weather.

" We made Carey's Swan's Nest on the 31st, in longitude
83° W., and latitude 62°, forty leagues from the north end
of Mansel's Isle; having thick, foggy weather, blowing hard,
the wind easterly and on the shore, could not try the tides,
or make bold with the land. Off this place I held a council,
where it was unanimously agreed to repair to Churchill
River, for reasons given in my journal, to which I refer your
lordship.

" August the 2nd it continued foggy; and meeting with
much ice, retarded us very much in our course. On the 7th,
made the land thirty miles to the eastward of Churchill
River, having had much ice, contrary winds, calms, and fogs,
for four days past. On the 9th, got both ships into Churchill
River, and employed our men in preparing winter quarters
for the ships, themselves, and provisions, by preparing an
old fort that was in ruins, cutting fire-wood to burn in the
long winter, digging a dock for the two ships, and places
under ground to secure our stores from the extreme frost.

" On the 31st hauled the two ships ashore, on account of the
spring tides, and to be out of the way of ice. September the
17th, got both ships securely moored, free from the dangers

of ice, and sent the men to their winter quarters. We had, for the most part, from the first of this month, hail, snow, and cold pinching weather; the land all covered with snow, and the shores lined with ice. The dock that we were obliged to dig for our ships was done with great labour and toil to our men night and day; had much ado to complete it before the winter came on, the ground being hard froze all the year, except three or four foot down, and many large stones and rocks we were obliged to blow up. By the 29th, the river was almost full of ice, and the northerly trade-winds set in, making it extreme cold. The wind blows between the N.N.E. and N.W. until the latter end of May. Most of our men employed in cutting wood for burning in stoves, which they haul home upon sledges over the frozen snow, when there is anything of moderate weather and they can stir abroad; for many days there is no looking out of doors, for the drifting snow and extreme frost.

" We continued four fires in our dwelling-house every day, in large brick stoves that will hold a good cart-load of wood each time; and at night, when burnt down, stop the top of the chimney to keep the heat in our apartments. After Christmas several of our men got the scurvy, with pains all over their limbs. By March they almost all had it, and several died. The frost is so extreme for four or five months in the winter, that we can hardly look abroad without freezing our faces, hands, or feet; and then lying in for cure brings on the scurvy; and whoever takes to his bed hardly ever gets abroad again, but falls into a looseness, which generally carries him off in eight or ten days. Though in twenty years that I have used this voyage, I never heard of, or knew, any afflicted with this, or any other distemper, before the last and this year.[1]

---

[1] This seems most unaccountable—unless it be the too free use of spirits, which may have occasioned so much illness on the present voyage.

"April the 7th, 1742. I ordered my officers and men to the ships (I mean such as were able to do anything, for we were very weak and sickly at that time), and employed them in clearing the ice from the inside of the ship, which was several inches thick, and airing the same with four or five large coal fires made in the iron stoves we had for that purpose. The carpenters were employed in fitting the ship for sea again; and about the middle of April set all hands to work in digging a dock in the ice to heave the ship farther astern before the river broke up; for the tides generally take off when the ice is gone. They worked with great labour night and day, as the tides would permit, in digging the dock and cutting the ice from the ship; but it was the 10th of June before I could get her into the river, where I laid her aground for the carpenters to bream and caulk. I have used the utmost despatch in getting both the ships ready for sea; and propose, if winds and weather permit, to sail this day, and diligently obey my instructions in proceeding on the voyage for the discovery of a passage from this place to the South Sea. And therefore wishing your lordship health and long life, beg leave to subscribe myself,

Right Hon. Sir,

Your most obedient and most humble servant,

(Signed)       CHRIST. MIDDLETON."

" *Furnace*, in Churchill River,
     June 28th, 1742."


" A little before the ships were ready for sailing, some Northern Indians came here to trade, and I prevailed on three of them, with presents and promises, to accompany me in my voyage. Two of these Indians speak several dialects of the Indian tongue, and have, as far as I can understand, been at Ne Ultra. The third is one who was brought up about the factory here, but has been among the Northern Indians, speaks their language and English tolerably well, and I hope will be of great service to the main design. I have herewith inclosed the observations I made here this winter.

"Sir Charles Wager, Knt."

The next letter I find from Captain Middleton reports his return to England on the 2nd October 1742, and encloses a continuation of his "Abstract of Proceedings".

"Hon. Sir,—I send this to acquaint you, for their lordships' information, that I am now working up the river Thames, in order to moor at Galleon's Reach, there to wait further orders. In this is inclosed an abstract of my proceedings in the voyage I was ordered upon ; and if their lordships would give me leave (at the return of this messenger I have sent) I shall wait upon them with a draught of the parts discovered, and a continuation of my journal from the 28th of June last till this time.

I am, Hon. Sir,

Your most obedient humble servant,

(Signed)                         Christ. Middleton."

"*Furnace*, at the Hope,
Oct. 2nd. 1742."

---

*An Abstract of the Proceedings of His Majesty's Ship*
*"Furnace", upon the Discovery, etc.*

" I sailed from Churchill the first day of July 1742, being the first spurt of wind I could get for sailing out of the harbour, and continued sailing with a fair wind till the 3rd,

16

when we saw an island, the two extremities bearing N. by E.
and E. by N., lying in the latitude of 63° 00′ N., and longitude from Churchill 3° 40′ E.; which I take to be the same
Fox named Brook Cobham.   On the fifth day I saw a headland on the north side of the Welcome, bearing N.W. by N.,
distant seven or eight leagues, in the latitude of 63° 20′, and
longitude from Churchill 4° 00′ E.   Here I tried the tides
several times, and found, close in with the land, the tide to
run two miles an hour from the N. by E., which I take to
be the flood; and by the slacks, from several trials, I found
that a west or W. by N. moon made high water, having a
full moon that day.   On the 8th saw the north side of the
Welcome, with much ice in shore.   I tried the tide, and
found it set E.N.E. two fathoms.   On the 9th, continuing
my course, and sailing through much ice, I was at length
obliged to grapple to a large piece.   The tender did the
same, to keep off from the shore, the wind blowing us right
upon it.   I tried the tide frequently, and could not discover
either ebb or flood by my current log.   Here we were fast
jammed up in ice, being totally surrounded for many miles,
and the wind setting it right upon us : it was all ice for ten
leagues to windward, and were in great danger of being
forced on shore ; but it happily falling calm after we had
lain in this condition two or three days, the pieces of ice
separated, or made small openings.   We being then within
two miles of the shore, and with no little difficulty hauled
the ships from one piece to another, till we got amongst what
we call sailing ice, that is, where there are such intervals of
water as a ship, by several traverses, may get forwards
towards the intended course.   In this manner we continued
till we saw a fine cape or headland to the northward of Whale
Bone Point, in the latitude of 65° 10′ N., and longitude from
Churchill, 8° 54′ E.   This I named, after my worthy[1] friend,

---

[1] *Un*worthy would have been more appropriate, for I cannot but think
he behaved very ill to Captain Middleton.—ED.

Cape Dobbs. I had very good soundings between the two shores of the Welcome, having forty-six, forty-eight, and forty-nine fathoms of water.

"At the same time that I saw Cape Dobbs, I descried a fair opening bearing N.W., which, according to my instructions, I stood in for amongst the sailing ice. It was just flood when we entered it, the tide running very strong; which, by observations afterwards, I found to run five or six miles an hour. I run over some rocks on the north side of it very luckily, being just high water, and anchored in about thirty-four fathom water; but when the tide of ebb was made, it ran so strong, and such quantities and bodies of ice came down upon us, that we were obliged to steer the ship all the time, and to keep all hands upon their guard with ice-poles to shove off the ice; notwithstanding which, it brought our anchor home, and taking hold again, one of the arms was broke off. The next day I sent my lieutenant in the boat to seek out some securer place for the ships, it being impossible to keep afloat long where we were. Some Usquemay savages came off to us, but had nothing to trade. I used them civilly, made them some presents, and dismissed them. As soon as I got the ships secured, I employed all my officers and boats, having myself no little share in the labour, in trying the tides, and discovering the course and nature of this opening; and after repeated trials, for three weeks successively, I found the flood constantly to come from the eastward, and that it was a large river we were got into, but so full of ice there was no stirring the ships with any probability of safety while the ice was driving up and down with the strong tides. Here I lay, not a little impatient to get out; went several times in my boat towards the mouth of the river, and from a hill that overlooked part of the Welcome, saw that place full of ice, so that I found that there was no time lost by our being in security. However,

I sent my lieutenant and master in the eight-oared boat, to
look out for a harbour near the entrance of the river, and it
was a small miracle that they got on board again, for they
were so jammed up with ice, which, driving with the strong
tides, would inevitably have stove the boat to pieces, and all
must have perished, had it not been for an opening in a
large piece, into which they got the boat, and with it drove
out of the river's mouth ; but when the tide slacked, the ice
opened as usual, and then they rowed over to the north
shore, so got in with the flood. I several times sent the
Indians ashore to see if they knew anything of the country,
but they were quite ignorant of it. In this vexatious condition I continued for three weeks, resolving to get out the
first opportunity the river was anything clear of ice, and
make what discoveries I could by meeting the flood tide.
This river, which, by my frequent trials of the lands,
soundings, tides, etc., I was able to take a draught of, I
named the River Wager, after the Right Hon. Sir Charles
Wager, etc.

  " On the 3rd of August the river, for the first time, was a
little clear of ice, and accordingly I sailed out of it in pursuit
of our discovery, and on the 5th, by noon, got into the latitude of 66° 14'. We had then got into a new strait much
pestered with ice, and on the north side of which we saw a
cape or headland bearing north. We had deep water and
very strong tides within four or five leagues of it. I named
this headland Cape Hope, as it gave us all great joy and
hopes of its being the extreme north part of America, seeing
little or no land to the northward of it. We turned or worked
round it the same night, and got five or six leagues to the
N. by W. before we could perceive any otherwise than a
fair and wide opening ; but about noon, the 6th day, after
having got into the latitude of 66° 40', found we were im-
bayed, and by two in the afternoon could not go above three

leagues farther ; and having tried the tides all the forenoon,
every two hours, till two o'clock in the afternoon, found
neither ebb or flood, yet deep water.  From this it was concluded that we had overshot the straits on the north-east
shore, from whence the flood came ; and as there was no
proceeding above three or four leagues farther, it was agreed
upon by all to return back, and search narrowly for a strait
or opening near where we found the strong tides.  On the
7th, after we were confirmed the flood came in on the north-
east side from the E. by S., I went on shore in the boat, and
found it flowed fifteen foot three days after the full, and a
W. by S. moon made high water.  I travelled twelve or
fifteen miles inland till I came to a very high mountain, from
whence I plainly saw the strait or opening the flood came in
at ; and the mountain I stood upon being pretty near the
middle of this strait, I could see both ends of it ; but it was
all froze fast, from side to side, being about eighteen or
twenty leagues long, and six or seven broad, having many
small islands in the middle and sides of it, and very high
land on both sides.  But as there was no appearance of the
ice clearing this year, and near the 67th degree of latitude,
no anchoring the ships, being very deep water close to the
shore, and much large ice driving with the ebb and flood,
and but little room if thick weather should happen, which
we continually expect in those parts,—it was agreed upon in
council to make the best of our way out of this dangerous,
narrow strait, and to make observations between the 64th
and 62nd degree of latitude.  The Frozen Strait I take to
run towards that which Bylot named Cape Comfort, and the
bay where Fox had named a place Lord Weston's Portland.
It is in the latitude of 66° 40', and longitude 12° 19' E. from
Churchill.

" Pursuant to the resolution, we bore away, and tried the
tides on the other side of the Welcome, sounding and observing close in shore, but met with very little encourage-

ment. On the 11th of August, I once more saw the Island Brook Cobham, and continued trying the tide; still finding the flood came from the eastward, and by coasting along the Welcome, was certain of its being the mainland, though there are several black whales of the right whale-bone kind seen thereabouts; and there are several small islands and deep bays. I worked off and on by Brook Cobham, sent the two Northern Indians ashore upon the island, who, at their return, gave me to understand that it was not far from their country, and desired I would let them go home, being tired of the sea. I kept them with assurances that I would act according to my promise, and finding no probability of a passage in two or three days after, I gave them a small boat well fitted with sails and oars, the use of which they had been taught, and loaded it with fire-arms, powder, shot, hatchets, and everything desirable to them. They took their leave of me, and I sent another boat with them for water, which accompanied them ashore, the Southern Indian being with them. The Southern Indian, who was linguist for the Northern ones, returned with the boat. He had been accustomed to the English at the Factory; and being desirous of seeing England, and a willing handy man, I brought him with me. The same evening, which was the 15th of August, I bore away for England, thinking to have tried the tides at Carey's Swan's-ness, but could not fetch it. On the 20th, saw Mansel's Isle. On the 21st, Cape Diggs was in sight. On the 26th, made Cape Resolution, and arrived at Cairston, in the Isles of Orkney, the 15th of September, where I put several men sick ashore,—most of the companies of the two ships being very much afflicted with the scurvy and otherwise distempered,—I waited there to recruit my men after the fatigues of the voyage, and to impress hands to bring the ships safe to the River Thames. I sailed from the Orkneys the 24th of the same month, and having variable winds and weather, am now working up the River Thames to moor at

Galleon's Reach, there to wait farther orders. For the particulars of the voyage, I humbly refer their lordships to my
journal and draught.

(Signed) CHRISTOPHER MIDDLETON."

Probably no officer employed upon such an expedition
was more unfortunate in the selection of his crew than Captain Middleton. A great part of them were pressed into
the service; and the following letter will convey some idea
of the troublesome characters he had to deal with.

" HON. SIR,—I beg leave to acquaint you, for the information of my Lords Commissioners of the Admiralty, that this
day I received their lordships' order of the 15th instant, in
relation to the five men, who are thereby directed to be discharged into the *Cornwall ;* and, in answer thereto, I desire
their lordships may be acquainted, that I should have been
glad to have got rid of them long ago, and am only sorry
Captain Stapylton is to be troubled with such villains; for,
notwithstanding I have used them all the voyage with great
lenity and indulgence, and have ordered them near a third
more provisions than his majesty's allowance, they have
broke open and plundered almost every cask in the ship, by
which I am no small sufferer, and now have deserted the
ship under my command without any leave or notice, and
enticed all the common hands to do the same, who, I
believe, did not want much invitation; for certainly no ship
was ever pestered with such a set of rogues, most of them
having deserved hanging before they entered with me, and
not three seamen among the whole number of private men ;
so that had it not been for the officers, who, every one of
them, worked like common men, I should have found no
little difficulty to get the ships to England.

" I am now almost destitute of working hands, and humbly
beg their lordships would please to order the officers of the

yard here to supply me with men to get the ship cleared of
her stores and provisions, as I shall, according to their lordships' directions, discharge the five men mentioned in their
order.

I am, Hon. Sir,

Your most obedient humble servant,

(Signed)    CHRIST. MIDDLETON."

" *Furnace,* at Woolwich,
    Oct. 16th, 1742."

" Hon. Secretary Corbett."

The following " observations", made by Captain Middleton at the winter quarters in Churchill River, are also
obtained from the Records of the Admiralty, and will be
found to contain much curious and interesting matter.

OBSERVATIONS.

*The effects of cold ; together with observations of the longi-
tude, latitude, refraction of the atmosphere, and declination of the magnetic needle, at Prince of Wales's Fort,
Churchill River, in Hudson's Bay, North America.
By Christopher Middleton, commander of his majesty's
ship " Furnace", 1741-42.*

" I observed that the hares, rabbits, foxes, and partridges,
in September and the beginning of October, change their
native colour to a snowy white ; and that for six months, in
the severest part of the winter, I never saw any but what
were all white, except some foxes of a different sort, which
were grizzled, and some half red, half white.

" That lakes and standing waters, which are not above ten
or twelve foot deep, are froze to the ground in the winter,
and the fishes therein all perish.

" Yet in rivers near the sea, and lakes of a greater depth than ten or twelve feet, fishes are caught all the winter, by cutting holes through the ice down to the water, and therein putting lines and hooks. But if they are to be taken with nets, they cut several holes in a straight line the length of the net, and pass the net, with a stick fastened to the head-line, from hole to hole, till it reaches the utmost extent, and what fishes come to these holes for air are thereby entangled in the net, and the fish, as soon as brought into open air, are instantaneously froze as stiff as stock fish. The seamen like-wise freshen their salt provisions by cutting a large hole through the ice in the stream or tide of the river, which they do at the beginning of the winter, and keep it open all that season. In this hole they put their salt meat, and the minute it is immersed under water, it becomes pliable and soft, though before its immersion it was very hard froze.

" Beef, pork, mutton, and venison, that are killed at the beginning of the winter, are preserved by the frost for six or seven months entirely free from putrefaction, and prove tolerable good eating. Likewise geese, partridges, and other fowl, that are killed at the same time, and kept with their feathers on and guts in, require no other preservative but the frost to make them good wholesome eating, as long as the winter continues. All kinds of fish are preserved in the like manner.

" In large lakes and rivers the ice is sometimes broken by imprisoned vapours, and the rocks, trees, joists, and rafters of our buildings, are burst with a noise not less terrible than the firing off a great many guns together. The rocks which are split by the frost are hove up in great heaps, leaving large cavities behind, which I take to be caused by impri-soned watery vapours that require more room when froze than they occupy in their fluid state. Neither do I think it unaccountable that the frost should be able to tear up rocks and trees, and split the beams of our houses, when I consider

17

the great force and elasticity thereof. If beer or water is left in mugs, canns, bottles, nay, in copper pots, though they are put by our bedsides, in a severe night they are surely split to pieces before morning, not being able to withstand the expansive force of the inclosed ice.

" The air is filled with innumerable particles of ice, very sharp and angular, and plainly perceptible to the naked eye. I have several times this winter tried to make observations of some celestial bodies, particularly the emersions of the satellites of Jupiter, with reflecting and refracting telescopes; but the metals and glasses, by that time I could fix them to the object, were covered a quarter of an inch thick with ice, and thereby the object rendered indistinct, so that it is not without great difficulties that any observations can be taken.

" Bottles of strong beer, brandy, strong brine, spirits of wine, set out in the open air for three or four hours, freeze to solid ice. I have tried to get the sun's refraction here to every degree above the horizon with Elton's quadrant, but to no purpose, for the spirits froze almost as soon as brought into open air.

" The frost is never out of the ground ; how deep, we cannot be certain. We have dug down ten or twelve feet, and found the earth hard froze in the two summer months; and what moisture we find five or six feet down is white, like ice.

" The waters or rivers near the sea, where the current of the tide flows strong, doth not freeze above nine or ten foot deep.

" All the water we use for cooking, brewing, etc., is melted snow and ice; no spring is yet found free from freezing, though dug never so deep down. All waters inland are froze fast by the beginning of October, and continue so till the middle of May.

" The walls of the house we live in are of stone, two foot

thick; the windows very small, with thick wooden shutters, which are close shut eighteen hours every day in the winter. There are cellars under the house, wherein we put our wines, brandy, strong beer, butter, cheese, etc. Four large fires are made in great stoves, built on purpose, every day. As soon as the wood is burnt down to a coal, the tops of the chimneys are close stopped with an iron cover. This keeps the heat within the house (though at the same time the smoke makes our heads ache, and is very offensive and unwholesome); notwithstanding which, in four or five hours after the fire is out, the inside of the walls of our house and bed places will be two or three inches thick with ice, which is every morning cut away with a hatchet. Three or four times a day we make iron shot of twenty-four pounds weight red hot, and hang them up in the windows of our apartments. I have a good fire in my room the major part of the twenty-four hours, yet all this will not preserve my beer, wine, ink, etc. from freezing.

" For our winter dress, we make use of three pair of socks of coarse blanketting or Duffield for the feet, with a pair of deer-skin shoes over them; two pair of thick English stockings, and a pair of cloth stockings upon them; breeches lined with flannel; two or three English jackets, and a fur or leather gown over them; a large beaver cap, double, to come over the face and shoulders, and a cloth of blanketting under the chin; with yarn gloves, and a large pair of beaver mittens hanging down from the shoulders before, to put our hands in, which reach up as high as our elbows: yet, notwithstanding this warm clothing, almost every day some of the men that stir abroad, if any wind blows to the northward, are dreadfully froze; some have their arms, hands, and faces, blistered and froze in a terrible manner, the skin coming off soon after they enter a warm house, and some have lost their toes. Now their lying in for the cure of these frozen parts brings on the scurvy in a lamentable manner. Many have died of it, and few are free from that distemper. I have procured them all the helps I could from the diet this country affords in winter,—such as fresh fish, partridges, broths, etc.,—and the doctors have used their utmost skill in vain; for I find nothing will prevent that distemper from being mortal but exercise and stirring abroad.

" I also find the effects of cold occasion a great error in the time of the sun's rising and setting, making the refraction of the atmosphere much greater than in Europe.

" I have observed the apparent time of the sun's central rising and setting for five or six months in the winter with a good level three or four days in a week. I had a good second watch of Mr. George Graham's for the time ; having computed the sun's true place, thence his declination, at the time when such appearance happened, and found his apparent rising sooner than the true time by near eight minutes, and his setting apparently so much later, so that the apparent day is longer than the real or astronomical day by almost sixteen minutes, and consequently the apparent night is so much shorter than the true night, making the horizontal refraction more than a degree. And as the refraction occasions an error in the time of the sun's rising and setting, so it likewise vitiates the amplitude; and this must be precisely heeded by mariners, or they will never gain the declination of the magnetic needle with any certainty, a thing of no small use and importance in the art of navigation.

" N.B. I used a level, by reason these observations were taken upon a place forty feet above the surface of the ocean, and about seven or eight feet above all the land in the way of the sun's rising and setting in the middle of winter.

" I am surprised those learned gentlemen, the French astronomers, who were sent from the Academy of Paris to the polar parts to observe and measure the figure of the earth, should find the refraction of the atmosphere to be no more than in France or England, when they complain of such extreme cold, and certainly not without reason.

" Coronæ and parhelia, commonly called halos and mock suns, appear frequently about the sun and moon here. They are seen once or twice a week about the sun, and once or twice a month about the moon, for four or five months in the winter; several of different diameters appearing at the same time.

" I have seen five or six parallel coronas concentric with the sun several times in the winter, being for the most part very bright, and always attended with halos or mock suns. The parhelia are always accompanied with coronas if the weather is clear, and continue for several days together, from the sun's rising to his setting. These rings are of various colours, and about forty or fifty degrees in diameter.

" The frequent appearance of these phenomena in this frozen clime seems to confirm Des-Carte's hypothesis, who supposes them to proceed from ice suspended in the air.

" The aurora borealis is much oftener seen here than in England; seldom a night passes in the winter free from their appearance. They shine with a surprising brightness, darkening all the stars and planets, and covering the whole hemisphere; their tremulous motion from all parts, their beauty and lustre, are much the same as in the northern parts of Scotland and Denmark, etc.

" The dreadful long winters here may almost be compared to the polar parts, where the absence of the sun continues for six months; for though we have that luminary here all the twelve months, yet the air is perpetually chilled and frozen by the northerly winds in winter, and the cold fogs and mists obstructing the sun's beams in the short summer we have here; for, notwithstanding the snow and ice is then dissolved in the low lands and plains, yet the mountains are perpetually covered with snow, and incredible large bodies of ice in the adjacent seas. If the air blows from the southern parts, the air is tolerably warm, but very cold when it comes from the northward, and it seldom blows otherwise than between the N.E. and N.W., except in the two summer months, when we have for the major part light gales between the east and the north, and calms.

" The northerly winds being so extreme cold is owing to the neighbourhood of high mountains, whose tops are perpetually covered with snow, which exceedingly chills the air passing over them. The fogs and mists that are brought here from the polar parts, in winter, appear visible to the naked eye in icicles innumerable, as small as fine hairs or threads, and pointed as sharp as needles. These icicles lodge on our clothes, and if our faces or hands be uncovered, they presently raise blisters as white as a linen cloth and as hard as horn; yet if we immediately turn our backs to the weather, and can bear our hand out of our mitten, and with it rub the blistered part for a small time, we sometimes bring the skin to its former state ; if not, we make the best of our way to a fire, and get warm water, wherewith we bathe it, and thereby dissipate the humours raised by the frozen air, otherwise the skin would be off in a short time, with much hot, serous, watery matter coming from under along with the skin. And this happens to some almost every time they go abroad, for five or six months, in the winter, so extreme cold is the air when the wind blows anything strong.

" Now I have observed, that when it has been extreme hard frost by the thermometer, and little or no wind that day, the cold has not near so sensibly affected us[1] as when the thermometer has shewn much less freezing, having a brisk gale of northerly wind at the same time. This difference may perhaps be occasioned by those sharp-pointed icicles, before-mentioned, striking more forcibly in a windy day than in calm weather, thereby penetrating the naked skin, or parts but thinly covered, and causing an acute sensa-

---

[1] Sir Edward Parry makes a precisely similar remark.

tion of pain or cold. And the same reason, I think, will hold
good in other places; for should the wind blow northerly
anything hard for many days together in England, the icicles
that would be brought from the polar parts by the continuance of such a wind, would, though imperceptible to the
naked eye, more sensibly affect the naked skin, or parts but
slightly covered, than when the thermometer has shewn a
greater degree of freezing, and there has been little or no
wind at the same time.

" It is not a little surprising to many, that such extreme
cold should be felt in these parts of America more than in
places of the same latitude on the coast of Norway; but the
difference I take to be occasioned by wind blowing constantly here, for seven months in the twelve, between the
N.E. and N.W., and passing over a large tract of land
and exceeding high mountains, etc., as before mentioned.
Whereas at Drunton,[1] in Norway, as I observed some years
ago in wintering there, the wind all the winter comes from
the north and N.N.W., and crosses a great part of the ocean
clear of those large bodies of ice we find here perpetually.
At this place we have constantly every year nine months'
frost and snow, and unsufferable cold from October till the
beginning of May. In the long winter, as the air becomes
less ponderous towards the polar parts, and nearer to an
æquilibrium, as it happens about one day in a week, we
then have calms and light airs all round the compass, continuing sometimes twenty-four hours, and then back to its old
place again, in the same manner as it happens every night
in the West Indies, near some of the islands.

" The snow that falls here is as fine as dust, but never any
hail, except at the beginning and end of winter. Almost
every full and change of the moon very hard gales from the
north.

" The constant trade-winds in these northern parts, I think

[1] Trondhjem, or Drontheim.

undoubtedly to proceed from the same principle which our learned Dr. Halley conceives to be the cause of the trade-winds near the equator, and their variations.

" 'Wind,' says he, ' is most properly defined to be the stream or current of the air ; and where such current is perpetual, and fixed in its course, 'tis necessary that it proceed from a permanent and unintermitting cause, capable of producing a like constant effect, and agreeable to the known properties of air and water, and the laws of motion of fluid bodies. Such an one is, I conceive, the action of the sun's beams upon the air and water, as he passes every day over the oceans, considered together with the nature of the soil and situation of the adjoining continents. I say, therefore, first, that according to the laws of statics, the air, which is less rarified or expanded by heat, and consequently more ponderous, must have a motion towards those parts thereof which are more rarified and less ponderous, to bring it to an æquilibrium,' etc.

" Now that the cold dense air, by reason of its great gravity, continually presses from the polar parts towards the equator, where the air is more rarified, to preserve an æquilibrium, or balance of the atmosphere, I think is very evident from the wind in those frozen regions blowing from the north and north-west from the beginning of October until May ; for we find that when the sun at the beginning of June has warmed those countries to the northward, then the south-east-east and variable winds continue till October again ; and I don't doubt but the trade winds and hard gales may be found in the southern polar parts to blow towards the equator, when the sun is in the northern signs, from the same principle.

" The limit of these winds from the polar parts towards the equator is seldom known to reach beyond the thirtieth degree of latitude, and the nearer they approach to that limit, the shorter is the continuance of those winds. In

New England it blows from the north near four months in the winter; at Canada about five months; at the Dane's Settlement in Strait Davis, in the sixty-third degree of latitude, near seven months; on the coast of Norway, in 64°, not above five months and a half, by reason of blowing over a great part of the ocean, as was before mentioned, for those northerly winds continue a longer or shorter space of time, according to the air's being more or less rarified, which may very probably be altered several degrees, by the nature of the soil, and the situation of the adjoining continent.

"The vast bodies of ice we meet with in our passage from England to Hudson's Bay is very surprising, not only as to quantity, but magnitude, and as unaccountable how they are formed of so great a bulk, some of them being immersed one hundred fathom or more under the surface of the ocean, and a fifth or sixth part above, and three or four miles in circumference. Some hundreds of these we sometimes see in our voyages here, all in sight at once, if the weather is clear. Some of them are frequently seen on the coasts and banks of Newfoundland and New England, though much diminished.

"When I have been becalmed in Hudson's Strait for three or four tides together, I have taken my boat and laid close to the side of one of them, sounded and found one hundred fathom water all round it. The tide floweth here above four fathom, and I have observed by marks upon a body of ice the tide to rise and fall that difference, which was a certainty of its being aground. Likewise, in a harbour in the Island of Resolution, where I continued four days, three of these isles of ice (as we call them) came aground: I sounded along by the side of one of them, quite round it, and found thirty-two fathom water, and the height above the surface but ten yards; another was twenty-eight fathom under, and the perpendicular height but nine yards above the water.

18

" I can in no other manner account for the aggregation of
such large bodies of ice but this. All along the coasts of
Straits Davis, both sides of Baffin's Bay, Hudson's Straits,
Anticosti, or Labrador, the land is very high and bold, and
one hundred fathoms or more close to the shore. These
shores have many inlets or fuirs,[1] the cavities of which are
filled up with ice and snow by the almost perpetual winters
there, and froze to the ground, increasing for four, five, or
seven years, till a kind of deluge or land flood, which commonly happens in that space of time throughout those parts,
breaks them loose, and launches them into the straits or
ocean, where they are drove about by the variable winds
and currents in the months of June, July, and August,
rather increasing than diminishing in bulk, being surrounded
(except in four or five points of the compass) with smaller
ice for many hundred leagues, and land covered all the year
with snow, the weather being extreme cold for the most
part in those summer months. The smaller ice that almost
fills the straits and bays, and covers many leagues out into
the ocean along the coast, is from four to ten fathom thick,
and chills the air to that degree, that there is a constant
increase to the large isles by the sea washing against them,
and the perpetual wet fogs, like small rain, freezing as they
settle upon the ice ; and their being so deeply immersed
under water, and such a small part above, prevents the
wind having much power to move them; for though it
blows from the north-west quarter near nine months in the
twelve, and consequently those isles are drove towards a
warmer climate, yet the progressive motion is so slow, that
it must take up many years before they can get five or six
hundred leagues to the southward ; I am of opinion some
hundreds of years are required, for they cannot, I think,
dissolve before they come between the fiftieth and fortieth
degree of latitude, where the heat of the sun consuming the

----

[1] Firths or fiords.

upper parts, they lighten and waste in time. Yet there is a
perpetual supply from the northern parts, which will so
continue as long as it pleases the Author of all Beings to
keep things in their present state.

*" Observations of the longitude, latitude, and the declination
of the magnetic needle, at Prince of Wales's Fort,
Churchill River.*

|  | | H. | ' | " |
|---|---|---|---|---|
| *" March the 20th, 1741-2.* | The true time of the emersion of the first satellite of Jupiter at London, according to Mr. Pound's tables. . | 18 | 23 | 50 |
| | The true time of the emersion at Churchill. . . . . . | 11 | 55 | 50 |
| | The horary difference of meridians. . | 6 | 28 | 00 |

"Which converted into degrees of the equator, gives
ninety-seven degrees, the distance of the meridian of Churchill from that at London. Wherefore, since the time at
London was more than that at Churchill (according to this
observation), Churchill must be ninety-seven degrees west
from London.

" I took several other observations, which agreed one with
another to less than a minute, but this I look upon as the
most distinct and best.

" The observation was made with a good fifteen-foot refracting telescope, and a two-foot reflector of Gregory's
kind, having a good watch of Mr. Graham's that I could
depend upon; for I had frequent opportunities of discovering how much its variation amounted to, and constantly
found its daily deviation or error to be fifteen seconds too
slow, by which means it was as useful to me for all purposes
as if it had gone most constantly true without any change.
This watch I kept in my fob in the day, and in bed in

the night, to preserve it from the severity of the weather, for I observed that all other watches spoiled by the extreme cold.

"I have found, from repeated observations, a method of obtaining the true time of the day at sea, by taking eight or ten different altitudes of the sun or stars when near the prime vertical, by Mr. Smith's or Mr. Hadley's quadrant, which I have practised these three or four years past, and never found from the calculations that they differed one from another more than ten or fifteen seconds of time. This certainty of the true time at sea is of greater use in the practice of navigation than may appear at first sight, for you thereby not only get the variation of the compass without the help of altitudes, but likewise the variation of the needle from the true meridian, every time the sun or star is seen to transit the same. Also having the true time, day or night, you may be sure of the meridian altitude of the sun or star, if you get a sight fifteen or twenty minutes before or after it passes the meridian, and the latitude may be obtained to less than five minutes, with several other uses in astronomical observations; as the refraction of the atmosphere, and to allow for it, by getting the sun's apparent rising and setting, which anybody is capable of doing, and from thence you will have the refraction.

"If we had such a telescope contrived as Mr. Smith recommends to be used on ship-board at sea, now we can have an exact knowledge of the true time of the day or night from the above instruments and a good watch; I hope we should be able to observe the eclipses of the first satellite of Jupiter, or any other phœnomena of the like kind, and thereby find the distance of meridians or longitude at sea.

"The variation of the magnetical needle, or sea compass, observed by me at Churchill in 1725 (as in No. 393 of the *Philosophical Transactions* for the months of March and April 1726), was at that time north 21° westerly, and this winter I have carefully observed it at the same place, and find it no more than 17°, so that it has differed about one degree in four years; for in 1738, I observed it here, and found its declination 18° westerly. I have carefully observed, and made proper allowance for the sun's declination and refraction, and find the latitude here to be 58° 56′ north; but in most parts of the world, where the latitudes are fixed by seamen, they are for the most part falsely laid down, for want of having regard to the variation of the sun's declination, which computed at a distant meridian, when the sun is near the equator, may make a great error in the sun's rising and setting, azimuths, etc.

" These things I thought proper to take notice of, as they may be of service to navigators, and the curious in natural inquiries."

CHRISTOPHER MIDDLETON.

FINIS.

# INDEX.